From Under My Brim

Stories from the California Coast Ranges

Ranger Barry Breckling

Jean,
Happy Trails
Barry

Published by
The Pine Ridge Association
of Henry W. Coe State Park

An alternate version of this book
is available on request
for people who find the print
difficult to read.

ISBN 0-97007-5-8

The Pine Ridge Association
9100 East Dunne Avenue
Morgan Hill, California 95037

Contents

Forward   4

Acknowledgements   7

Credits   9

Room to Roam   11

Prairie Wolves   22

Fire   29

Life's Blood   35

Spring Fever   41

Life on the Pine Ridge Ranch   48

Life in an Oak Tree   55

Something Stinks in Here   65

Pronghorn   69

The Monument Pine   75

Sometimes Things Just Fall into Place   79

Spring   83

The Emerald Chain   93

The Legend of the Oak   99

Forward

"Sometimes things just fall into place." Such a fortuitous event occurred more than a quarter century ago, when Ranger Barry Breckling came to Henry W. Coe State Park. Through the uniformed volunteer program that he started, many interpretive programs and training sessions each year, and daily interactions with the public, he has touched the lives of tens of thousands and deeply enriched the lives of thousands.

One of the ways in which he has entertained, taught, and moved people is through "From under My Brim," the lead article in each issue of *The Ponderosa* since 1979. This book contains his selection of a sampling of those articles. There are many more where these came from, as most years have had five issues.

Reading any of Barry's stories is a learning experience. One might be given a detailed vision of what daily life was like on the Coe Ranch ("Life on the Pine Ridge Ranch") or a loving description of some of Coe's prettiest spring wildflowers ("Spring"). Almost all of his writing concerns the vital inter-relations between plants and animals ("Life in an Oak Tree"), soil and rainfall ("Life's Blood"), and the vital cycle of life, which includes death, decay, and rebirth ("The Monument Pine"). His stories are most moving when he describes the harm that has been done to the environment and its creatures in recent centuries ("Fire") and the people, ancient and modern, who had the wisdom to regard nature with respect and appreciation ("Pronghorn"). The history and natural history are accurately described based on study and personal observations. But what makes his writing sing is the great amount of heart between every line.

As Barry concludes in "Spring":

> As I spent more time with the buttercup, I realized that its existence was just as important as the existence of an ant, a sequoia, or any other living thing. I gained more respect for all life and more insight into my connection with the buttercup and all the other inhabitants of this earth.

Kevin Gilmartin

4

❖ ❖ ❖ ❖ ❖ ❖ ❖ ❖ ❖ ❖ ❖

My first contact with Ranger Barry Breckling was in 1982. The world seemed simple back then—those were the days before computers, e-mail, and spam. My husband Kevin and I had just taken up backpacking, and we were looking for nearby parks where we could hike and camp. When looking at a map, we found a large green area outside Morgan Hill, which looked like a possible candidate. I wrote a letter of inquiry to the park, and received a prompt reply from Barry. He provided suggestions for several backpacking routes and included a map on which he had thoughtfully highlighted the suggested hikes. He concluded by suggesting that, while we may have been used to hiking long distances in other parks, the miles were much longer in Coe Park. Our first backpack trip at Coe, while memorable (as it motivated us to come back often over the past 22 years!), was not nearly as memorable as our friendship with Barry over the past 15-plus years.

Barry is in his element when he can teach, but he does it in such a way that you often don't realize that this is what he is doing. He loves to share Nature with others; he has given descriptions of a new spring wildflower to park visitors that are so detailed that any one could recognize it on the trail when they saw it. He has a knack for finding out what you enjoy learning about, and he goes out of his way to share information about that with you. For example, he took us to see a wonderful killdeer nest in the Orestimba, so that we could see how very invisible the eggs appeared against the rocks of the creek bed—something we had read about for years but had never seen firsthand.

His teaching continues in his stories. He challenges us to live more closely with the earth ("Fire"). He teaches us about the natural world around us by using lichens as an example ("Life in an Oak Tree"). He shows us the web of life—how all life is connected, from mistletoe, to the birds, to the oaks. He points out the importance of the balance of nature—how everything has a part to play, whether it be fire or acorns. He makes us think about what nature has to offer us now and what the natural world might look like after we humans put sickness and death on the earth when we are not attuned to the earth ("Life's Blood").

He concludes that we humans have a choice—it is up to us what we do—whether to live in harmony with the land and protect it or undercut it so that it dies.

Let us do as Barry suggests in "Prairie Wolves:" "Be quiet and listen.... You might just learn something."

Barbara Bessey

Acknowledgements

First I want to thank my wife, Judy. She has edited all my later "brims" and this book, and she's done so much cleanup work on my stories that she could be considered a coauthor. It's amazing that after she slashes my stories and we battle over the finished product, we are still best friends. Of course, she always insists that the final decision is mine.

I owe a debt of gratitude to Dan McCranie, who played a huge part in getting this book to progress from an idea to a reality.

I would also like to thank two great friends who encouraged me in a number of ways, Winslow Briggs and Lee Sims. All three of us were working on books at the same time but making little progress. Winslow was preparing an anthology of Sada Coe's stories, Lee was working on his tree book, and I was working on this book. The main encouragement they gave me was in the form of a bet. We each put some bucks in an envelope, and after six months, more bucks. The winner of the envelope would be the person who got his book onto the shelves of the PRA bookstore first. Who got the envelope? You'll have to ask Winslow or Lee.

Finally, I'd like to thank the fine artists who donated their work for this book, with a special thanks to Kathy Paivinen for her beautiful cover artwork.

Credits

Copyrights for the photos and artwork in this book are held by the people listed below. (Page numbers are in parentheses.)

Robert Buchner: Outhouse under oak (65)

Stew Eastman: Coyotes (24 and 26)

Teddy Goodrich: Orestimba Creek (36), Mississippi Lake (37)

Rosse Hemeon: Ranch house (48), white barn (50), cooler (53)

Dave Hildebrand: Mushroom (58)

Don Mason: Monument pine (75)

Judy Mason: Coyote (22), coast live oak (57), valley oak (60), blue oak (60), lion track (81), iris (89), purple mouse-ears (89)

Dan McCranie: Stetson hat (1), Indian (27), bobcat and mouse (45), skunk (67), bow with feather (71), acorn woodpecker (76), downed wood (78), rattlesnake (93)

Kathy Paivinen: Ranger hat cornucopia (front cover), acorn woodpecker (59), lion (79), lion skull (80), buttercup (92)

Rosemary Rideout: Brook (38)

Dave Sellers: Grizzly and cubs (13)

Chris Weske: Smoke (29)

Barry Breckling: Arrow (15), spur (17), rifle (20), smoke (31), feather (34), clouds (35), computer (41) thunderhead clouds (43), Johnny-jump-up (46), oak silhouette (55), galls (58), scrub jay (61), oak silhouette (62), lion figurine (82), manzanita (84), oak titmouse (85), Johnny-jump-up (87), two-eyed violet (88), acorns (99 and 100), sunset reflection (back cover)

The following wildflower illustrations are by Margaret Warriner Buck from *The Wild Flowers of California* by Mary Elizabeth Parsons, 1955, California Academy of Sciences, San Francisco: poppy (83), milkmaid (85), shooting star (86), delphinium (87), columbine (88), California gilia (90), mariposa lily (91).

Pronghorn (69) is from *Wood's Popular Natural History* by J. G. Wood, 1885.

"The Last California Grizzly" from *The Pine Ridge Country*, copyright Sada Sutcliffe Coe. Permission for use provided by Irene Lim and Bonnie Nazarenko (18-20).

Room to Roam

Room to Roam

At the turn of the twentieth century, there were few grizzly bears left in California. The surviving grizzlies inhabited rugged territories that were too remote to be of interest to the endless waves of human immigrants who took up residence in the state. Most of the grizzlies in the Sierra Nevada were wiped out earlier than grizzlies in other parts of the state because of the gold rush and the hordes of people it brought to the mountains.

Nevertheless, Tracy I. Storer and Lloyd P. Tevis, Jr., in their book The California Grizzly, *reported that the last sighting of a California grizzly bear was in Sequoia National Park in 1924.*

As the number of grizzlies decreased and the motivation to wipe them out increased, it was inevitable that different stories would evolve about the last grizzly bear in California. According to the story passed down to Sada Coe, the last California grizzly was killed in a "wild and remote" part of the south Mount Hamilton Range in 1910. The Hamilton Range in the early 1900's was certainly a rugged, isolated area where grizzlies made a last stand.

People may find it ironic that a state with no grizzly bears has a grizzly on its state flag, on its state seal, and on the shoulder patches of state park rangers.

❖ ❖ ❖ ❖ ❖ ❖ ❖ ❖ ❖ ❖

She feared nothing in her realm, not even men with guns. But she'd become wise over the years and had learned to avoid humans as much as possible. She was the last California grizzly in the Coast Ranges.

One morning, she approached a familiar meadow, traveling along a hillside trail that she and her ancestors had used for hundreds of years. In areas that stayed wet during the winter months, the trail was marked by evenly spaced holes up to eight inches deep. She and her forebears had formed the holes by stepping in the same spots year after year. Her two cubs tried as hard as they could to keep up with her, but they had a rough time of it with their shorter stride. In the middle of the meadow, not far from the creek, she paused and contemplated a large limb that had fallen from a sprawling old valley oak. She rolled the limb over with her left arm and with her right paw quickly snatched a meadow mouse as it dashed out. She devoured the mouse and then began to rip open the decaying underside of the log. She spotted a succulent white grub, delicately picked it up between two of her claws, and sucked it into her salivating mouth.

She dug deep into the duff close to the limb and unearthed a millipede. Lowering her head, she gently picked up the squirming creature with her lips and swallowed it whole. Following her example, the cubs also dug here and there and ate what they could find, but they were more interested in play and spent most of their time romping around. Every now and then, they bumped into their mother or rolled under her body, but with her thick layers of fat and her concentration focused on finding tidbits to eat, she scarcely noticed them.

After a while, the cubs ran out of energy and fell asleep at the base of the big oak tree, one on top of the other, a position they often took on top of their tolerant mother when she lay down to rest.

As her cubs dozed, she dug deep into moist dark soil and uncovered the broken thigh bone of a human being.

❖ ❖ ❖ ❖ ❖ ❖ ❖ ❖ ❖ ❖ ❖

Many years earlier, one of her ancestors had wandered into the same meadow one morning to search for food under the same oak tree. He was an adult male grizzly. He weighed almost a thousand pounds and he feared nothing. He certainly wasn't intimidated by the twelve dome-shaped, grass-covered huts close by. When the people who lived in the huts saw him, they dashed in every direction, and many of them headed for other trees at the edge of the meadow. They knew bears, and they knew that adult grizzlies couldn't climb trees, unlike the smaller, less aggressive black bears that were common farther north.

The people did not revere the grizzly as they did the coyote and the hummingbird. Instead, they regarded grizzlies with superstitious awe. Some of the people believed that grizzlies were actually humans, very evil humans with superior intelligence and supernatural powers.

The grizzly showed no interest in the frightened people as his nose led him from the sparse pickings under the tree to the row of granaries where the people stored their acorns. As he ripped through the first granary, one of the people shot an arrow at his massive body. The arrow lodged in the thick, grizzled fur of his left shoulder and slightly pierced his skin. He brushed the arrow away and began to devour acorns.

Some of the people continued to shoot arrows at him in a desperate attempt to save their acorn harvest. Two arrows penetrated his hide and aroused his wrath. He turned on his assailants, ran one of them down, knocked the man over, and broke his thigh bone with a single swipe. He pawed at the cowering human for a moment or two, but soon lost interest and returned to the acorns.

The immense bear lived for many more years, feeling little effect from the two arrowheads that remained embedded in his flesh. Although he continued to have occasional encounters with humans, he lived out his life with plenty of room in which to roam.

❖ ❖ ❖ ❖ ❖ ❖ ❖ ❖ ❖ ❖

When she'd consumed all the edible tidbits she could find in the area, she ambled off to the nearby creek and settled into a pool, not much bigger than she was, for a refreshing bath. She closed her eyes occasionally, but never lost awareness of her two cubs, who were still napping in the shade of the huge oak tree.

She and their father had met around the middle of June in the previous year and had parted in the early days of July. When summer turned to fall, she'd begun to anticipate the birth of her cubs. Each day she stayed a bit closer to a shallow cave beneath a rocky ledge, the site she had used as her den for most of her life.

She spent much of her time resting as fall turned to winter, but she didn't go into hibernation. Her relatives in the high mountains had to hibernate each year to survive the severe winter weather, but she lived in the milder climate of the Inner Coast Ranges, and she didn't need to hibernate.

On a rainy morning in January, she gave birth to two healthy ten-ounce cubs who were clothed in a fine, almost invisible coat of hair. Eventually, when they reached adulthood, they would be covered with a raggedy-looking mix of thick dark brown fur and long white-tipped "grizzled" guard hairs.
The sleeping cubs now weighed over 45 pounds. They'd taken advantage of the fall's abundance and had put on lots of fat. They awoke from their nap, stretched a little, and then joined their mother. Feeling a bit warm from their snuggled sleep, they tried to nudge their way into the cool water with her.
She slowly got up to make room for her cubs. As she stepped out of the pool, one of her paws dislodged something from the bank of earth alongside the creek. It was a tarnished old Spanish spur, with an eight-spoked rowel bent to one side.

❖ ❖ ❖ ❖ ❖ ❖ ❖ ❖ ❖ ❖ ❖

Many years back, her great grandfather had dashed down the open creek bed, trying to escape the riatas of six caballeros who pursued him on horseback. He knew that these people were dangerous. The year before, they had shot and killed three of his kind, and he'd barely escaped with a bullet in his hip.
One of the caballeros tossed a riata around the enormous bear's neck. The man's horse skidded to a stop, jerking the grizzly off of his feet and into the air. The bear landed on his back, creating a huge cloud of dust. Another lasso encircled

one of his feet, but he swung a powerful arm with sharp claws and snapped the rope off in an instant. He scrambled to his feet, turned, and ran toward the man at the other end of the 30-foot rope that had brought him down. He covered the distance with incredible speed, catching the man and his horse off guard. With no cue from her rider, the agile horse quickly veered to the left as the angry bear swung at her with one of his paws, just missing her chest and raking across the man's tapadero-covered stirrup.

The bear's claws had shredded the thick leather tapadero, ripped off the man's boot, and left bloody inch-deep lacerations across the side of his foot. Though the blow had lost most of its force when it reached the man's spur, it had torn the spur loose, bent the rowel, and sent the thing spinning into the air. The spur landed about 20 feet away, near the edge of the creek.

The bear's species would one day be given the name *Ursus horribilis*.

The caballeros eventually got three more lariats cinched tightly around the bear's limbs, and they dragged him for many miles before they reached civilization. A few days later the bear would be pitted against the largest, meanest bull in the valley. With luck, he might defeat the bull, but tethered by a chain, he'd be at a disadvantage, and at best would emerge a maimed and bloody victor.

The wild lands were shrinking, and the remaining bears would have less and less room in which to roam.

She shook the water off her thick coat with a crescendo of shaking that began slowly at her nose, gained speed and intensity as it moved toward her rear, and then tapered off to a little shake of her short tail. Her cubs waded out of the pool and, in unison, imitated her drying technique. The bear and her cubs wandered slowly downstream and then stopped when they spotted a small herd of sheep. The mother bear easily ran down a plump ewe and promptly dispatched her with a blow to her neck. The cubs caught up with their mother, and the three of them feasted on her prey until...

I'll let Sada Coe continue the story. In her book *The Pine Ridge Country*, she related the account that had been passed down to her about the last grizzly bear in California.

THE LAST CALIFORNIA GRIZZLY

She was the last remaining grizzly in the State of California, and in bewildered fear of her aloneness lived in the wild and remote part of the south Mount Hamilton Range. Slow and lumbering she hunted near her cave for food, never venturing very far from the great rocky ledge that climbed straight up from a narrow creek. Here in a thick timber of pines she made her home.

She had lost her nerve. It happened one year when she and her two half grown cubs were feasting on a tender sheep they had just killed. The old keeper and his dog found them suddenly and without warning slaughtered the two cubs. It was only luck she had been spared, but her heart was broken and old age weakened her strength. All the cattle people knew of her and a price was placed on her head as the last of her species to survive the white man. A horrible fear kept her from roaming the old haunts she once knew. The price was fifty dollars to the first man who brought her head to the valley, but only by shooting would the reward be gained and dogs or poison bait were forbidden in the chase. In spite of her past deeds the old cowmen felt a great respect for the aged grizzly.

A horse trader, however, living in the valley learned of the price of the grizzly's head, and as fifty dollars at the time was considered a small fortune, he set out to gain the prize. He rode far back into the hills until he found the tracks of the old bear where she had been foraging for food. Unable to catch her at a disadvantage, he decided at last to poison the great beast. No one would know, he thought, so taking a freshly killed deer, he applied a few grains of poison to the meat and then waited.

Lumbering along her usual haunt she smelled the fresh blood of the deer and soon came upon its carcass. Hungry and weakened by age, she ate the meat greedily. The poison quickly began its work and the great animal writhed in agony towards her cave, but death was quick and she died within a hundred yards of the deer. Here the horse trader found her, and to make sure that the prize would be his, fired a bullet from his rifle into the dead bear's head, which he then removed and took proudly back to the valley. There was a great excitement over the event, and he flourished for awhile with popularity and fame. Many years passed and after the man's death the true story then became known of the killing of the last California grizzly.

❖ ❖ ❖ ❖ ❖ ❖ ❖ ❖ ❖ ❖ ❖

A few years later, the horse trader persuaded a few people to ride along with him on a trip to the meadow so that he could impress them with a reenactment of his story. The small party of horsemen followed the hillside trail and began to descend to the meadow below.

Just above the creek, the horse trader whipped his Winchester from its sheath to demonstrate the "fateful shot." As he raised the rifle, his horse tripped in a set of deep holes and the gun flew into the air. The man was astonished. It seemed that the weapon had been struck from his grip.

He and his acquaintances searched for the rifle for a couple of hours. In their search, they ran across an old brittle piece of a human thigh bone and an old bent Spanish spur, but they never found the gun.

With each passing day, as the wild lands continue to shrink and wildlife disappears, more stories will be told of animals who have less and less room in which to roam.

Prairie Wolves

Humans have caused many animals to disappear from the face of the earth forever. Sometimes, we've destroyed species inadvertently. At other times, we've set out with deliberation and determination to annihilate a species. But we don't always succeed. Some species that we've tried to exterminate have managed to outwit us and have grown in strength and number.

❖ ❖ ❖ ❖ ❖ ❖ ❖ ❖ ❖ ❖

Jesse said, "Too bad you can't eat them prairie wolves. You know we've shot enough this year that we wouldn't have to eat no more of the sheep."

His brother Frank answered, "I don't think there was enough meat on all those flea-bitten, scroungy dogs put together to feed us for more than a day and a half."

Jesse shook his head in agreement and added, "There ain't no more despicable animal I know of than a prairie wolf. They look like a bunch of long, wobbly-jointed bones stuck in a fur coat that's a size too big and got so few hairs that a flea wouldn't live on them for fear he'd die of sunstroke."

Frank said, "Do you remember the one we saw a couple a weeks ago when we didn't have our rifles? It saw us and took off a runnin' with its tail dragging the ground. It kept lookin' over its shoulder at us with its evil eye and that smile that looked like he knew somethin' we didn't."

Jesse lit the kerosene lantern as the pink glow in the windows was almost gone. As the lantern's light filled the little one-room cabin, an most eerie howl came from somewhere nearby in the darkness outside. Jesse grabbed his rifle and said to Frank, "It sounds like there's a pack of them varmints out by the barn." Jesse ran out the door with one suspender over his torn long underwear and only holey socks on his feet. As he ran towards the barn, he tripped on a low pile of firewood and hit his head on the edge of the rock-encased well.

Frank was saying, "Wake up, wake up!" As Jesse opened his eyes, Frank repeated, "Wake up and pay attention to the professor." Jesse looked around and realized he was sitting in a college classroom. He wondered how this could be possible as he never even finished third grade.

The professor was saying, "Now we'll go on to the coyote, occasionally called brush wolf or prairie wolf. Its scientific name is *Canis latrans*, which means barking dog. Coyotes do have a wide

Prairie Wolves

variety of yips and howls, but they actually bark very little. The name 'coyote' comes from the word 'coyotl' of the Nahuatl language, and it was the Aztec name for the coyote. Coyotes are medium-sized canids weighing between 20 and 40 pounds, with occasional individuals reaching 50 pounds. They are about four feet long, including a tail that's about 16 inches long, and they stand about 18 to 20 inches at the shoulder. Their fur is generally gray in color but may vary towards a reddish-brown. They have rufous red hair on their feet, legs, and ears. A coyote's tail is tipped in black, and there is a black spot on the upper middle part of the tail and some black on their backs."

Jesse saw that he was taking notes, which he found very strange; as best he could remember, he couldn't read, much less write.

The professor continued, "Their ears are large and erect and they have a good sense of hearing, as well as an excellent sense of smell. They are omnivorous and will eat rodents, insects, berries, human garbage, and carrion. As a matter of fact, they will eat almost anything. Coyotes can run about 40 miles per hour, so they often use their speed to catch prey. They can also get into an easy trot that they can keep up for hours, which allows them to cover extensive territory in their search for food. Their home range can be a few thousand acres. Coyotes don't hunt in packs as do wolves. You may see family groups hunting together, but those groups technically are not packs. Coyotes typically mate for life. They usually dig their own dens, which can be up to 30 feet long and as much as six feet below the surface. The female gives birth in late spring to five or six and occasionally as many as ten young. Coyotes have been extensively hunted, trapped, and poisoned over the years. In one year during the 1960s, for example, 89,653 were killed."

Jesse thought, "I didn't know there were even that many animals in the whole United States. And how did we get to the 1960s anyway? I thought it was 1948!"

The professor went on, "In areas where coyotes are significantly reduced in number, rodent populations explode and become a problem for farmers and ranchers. In such areas, surviving coyotes respond to the slaughter by having larger litters, and they can quickly reinhabit areas from which they were removed. Before the arrival of Europeans, coyotes were confined to western America. Wolves, which need big game for food, were either killed outright or retreated due to the lack of food as humans killed off all the big game. Coyotes moved into the territory vacated by the wolves. They were able to survive on a more meager diet. Now they are found as far east as Pennsylvania and Maine, and they range north through western Canada to Alaska. Amazingly, coyotes are more numerous now than they were before humans started killing them off in large numbers. They are extremely resourceful animals. Coyotes even live in close proximity to humans, their only true enemy."

Prairie Wolves

That made sense to Jesse. It seemed the more he killed, the more there were. Jesse found himself mildly bored. After all, what in the heck did "proximity" mean. He started to doze off.

Jesse felt someone nudge him. "Pay attention grandson," a voice said. Jesse rubbed his eyes and saw that he was sitting on the ground in front of a fire. The old man sitting next to him was shirtless and barefooted. He was wearing only a deer skin, which was wrapped around his middle.

The old man looked Jesse straight in the eyes and said, "You know Coyote is full of trickery and magic and that he is the father of our people. He gave us the net and the bow and arrow, and he taught us how to make acorn mush. When all other animals are gone from the earth, Coyote will remain. You know he teaches us how to live. These things the elders taught you when you were just a young child. Grandson, what have you learned from Coyote?"

Jesse, with his mouth wide open, stared back at the old man and didn't utter a sound. Besides having no answer to the question, he had no idea where he was and who this old man could be.

The old man said, "Did you not learn that Coyote is a smart and beautiful animal? In the summer he is smart. He loses all his under fur and has just his long guard hairs. He stays cool. We have learned from Coyote not to wear a fur in the summer. In the winter he is covered with a beautiful thick fur that keeps him warm. He taught us to wear fur in the winter to keep warm.

Did you not learn that Coyote is a good husband and father? He stays with one wife and when the babies are born he brings food to the den to feed them. The mother cleans the den every day. It is never filthy.

Coyote can hunt by himself but likes the company of others. Did you not learn that Coyote is crafty and resourceful? He eats the grasshopper when it is plentiful, the mouse when it is foolish,

Prairie Wolves

the berries when they are ripe. He uses his great speed to run down the rabbit. Did you not see Coyote lie as if dead until the magpie came to look and then he quickly grabbed it? Did you not see Coyote chase the rabbit past the bush where his mate was waiting to take up the chase? Did you not see Coyote wait near the digging badger until the ground squirrel ran out and he grabbed it?

Our people are like Coyote because we have learned from him. When things are plentiful, we have much. When things are scarce, we use our wits and our wisdom and our deep desire to survive. At night Coyote talks to the Creator in the spirit world. Have you not heard his long clear call, the high-pitched barks and yaps, the mystical sounds that could only be praying? My grandson, I do not think you are yet a man. You have much to learn."

Jesse was embarrassed and very tired from this ordeal. He leaned his head on grandfather's lap and fell asleep.

Jesse awoke to the sound of his brother saying, "Can you hear me? Are you OK?" Jesse sat up but still felt dazed. He wasn't sure if it was from the blow to his head or his very lifelike dreams. Frank said, "Get your gun! Look there. One of them prairie wolves is on the ridge up there with the moon right behind him. It's an easy shot. Can't you hear him howlin' to the moon? Go on, shoot him! What's a matter with you?"

Jesse listened to the coyote howling and gazed at its silhouette. He picked up his rifle and threw it into the well, then turned to Frank and said, "Be quiet and listen.... You might just learn something."

Fire

We so often feel compelled to control things. We can do better than nature, we think. But we're almost always wrong.

❖ ❖ ❖ ❖ ❖ ❖ ❖ ❖ ❖ ❖

It looked like an early rain was going to dampen the woods and fields, but the clouds held more than just rain. Out of the billowing white clouds came lightning. One bolt struck a tall pine on the ridge top. Electricity spiraled down the trunk, and flames jumped up in the grass at the tree's base.

The rain, though heavy, was short lived and did little to stop the fire, which was quickly pushed forward by the strong wind. The flames burned much of a field of bunch grasses, but below the ground, the rootstocks survived. They would lie dormant until the winter rains came, and the new growth would be greener and stronger because of the nutrients that were released by the fire.

Fire

Flames blazed up through an old black oak, burning out much of the heartwood from the ground up to an old broken-off branch 20 feet in the air. The fire made a cavelike tunnel that would provide shelter for a fox, a raccoon, and a bobcat at various times during the next decade.

The fire swept through a grove of young, overcrowded pines that had begun life right after the last fire in the area, 15 years earlier. All the pines were killed, except for one that was healthier and slightly taller than its neighbors. Its lower branches would never see green needles again, but neither would they see flames when the next fire came through 12 years later. The fire burned halfway up an old 120-foot pine that had become seriously weakened by bark beetles. The cambium layer, nearly destroyed by the insects, was finished off by the fire, and the bark and all the bark beetles were consumed by the flames. The remaining needles soon died, but the tree continued to stand. It became a nesting site for kestrels and provided a home and acorn storage site for an extended family of acorn wood-peckers. A pair of red-tailed hawks used a dead branch as a place to perch and look for prey in years when the kestrels nested elsewhere.

As the fire spread through forest and field, the elk and grizzly, the deer and mountain lion all ran ahead of the flames to safety. The ground squirrel and badger, the mouse and weasel escaped death deep in their dens. The birds escaped into the air, and as a dark-eyed junco flew off, one of its white outer tail feathers drifted down and landed on the cooling ashes.

Nutrients released by the fire would bring an abundance of plant life to the area, which would in turn increase the number and vitality of the animals that reinhabited the area.

No one was there to put out the fire. It would burn and smolder and burn again for weeks in the cool days of late fall, and finally the rains would come and put it out completely...

❖ ❖ ❖ ❖ ❖ ❖ ❖ ❖ ❖ ❖ ❖

Lightning struck a tall pine on the ridge and a fire started.
First half an acre, then an acre, then two burned, but before
the fire could spread further, a helicopter dropped off six men
who started scraping a fire line around the east side. The heli-
copter left but quickly returned with water and "picked up" the
south side, and soon three air tankers dropped a red liquid that
put out the fire on the west side. Finally, a bulldozer arrived and
stopped the fire on the north side. All that remained for the
ground crew to do was to cut down a couple of burning snags.
Success!

Smokey the Bear would be proud. Another fire had been
conquered. In fact, with the exception of this small fire and two
that were even smaller, the area had not burned for over 90
years.

Fire

Three weeks later, the weather warmed and 30-mile-per-hour winds blew from out of the east. A hiker stopped at the top of the ridge, sat on a stump to have a smoke, and then flipped the cigarette butt to the edge of the road. The cigarette started some leaves smoldering and quickly the grass sparked into flames. In just minutes the fire had spread to 10 acres, then to 100, and before nightfall it had burned over 1,000 acres. (In the end, over 9,000 acres would be engulfed by the fire before it was finally extinguished.)

On a wooded slope, the flames burned up through thick brush and dead branches that had accumulated over the years. The brush and dead wood carried the fire with tremendous heat up into the tops of the oaks and pines, killing many of them. A fox that lived in a hollowed-out black oak died along with the tree. Although the deer ran with great speed, some were caught by the flames.

Heat in some areas was so extreme that it sterilized the soil, killing every seed buried near the surface. In a thick grove of 25-year-old pines, not one survived. Birds flew in all directions and most escaped. A crow, blinded by the smoke, crashed into the top of a burning tree, and black feathers flew. Only one feather escaped the flames, and it slowly drifted down to the ashes below...

❖ ❖ ❖ ❖ ❖ ❖ ❖ ❖ ❖ ❖

On Wednesday, November 4th, 1992, a fire crew walked Pine Ridge with drip torches, laying down lines of fire. Most of the area between the park headquarters and the Little Fork of the Coyote Creek had not burned since 1886 — 106 years earlier! This was not a controlled burn (we'd learned long ago how difficult it is to control the forces of nature); this was a prescribed burn, lit only when temperature, humidity, wind, fuel moisture, and soil moisture all fell within the ranges specified by the prescription.

I walked the area a week after the start of the fire, and I took a more extensive walk another week after that. On my second visit, I found some stumps still smoking and areas of leaf litter still smoldering. The burn had gone well; even the cool, damp, north-facing slopes had burned. A mosaic of burned and unburned areas was left behind. Although less intense than a natural fire, the prescribed fire did a fair job of cleaning out the sick, the old, and the dead.

What impressed me most though was how quickly the wildlife returned. Birds were everywhere. Bluebirds and a lone oak titmouse hopped around in the ashes picking up insects. Robins pretended to hide between quick grabs for madrone berries. A covey of quail scurried through the ashes from some surviving bushes to the protection of the limbs and leaves of a fire-felled black oak. Acorn woodpeckers were all around, mouthing off as usual and as happy as ever. I saw a hairy and a downy wood-pecker, and I'm sure I heard a Nuttall's. Two red-tailed hawks circled above, and throughout the burn area I saw Steller's and scrub jays going about their business.

From a distance, meadows seemed only black and gray with ash. But on closer inspection, I found green grass that had sprouted, even though there had been no rain since the fire. I discovered many seedlings already coming up, including several California poppy plants a few inches tall. On the shady slopes, bunch grasses were sprouting from their rootstocks. Pine thickets that were 10, 15, and even 20 years old were burned so completely that most were killed, but I could tell that a few would survive. I saw one large buck and a number of does with their offspring. Mice, voles, and ground squirrels were making new trails and had pushed out new earth on top of the ashes. A badger or two had dug several holes across the top of the ridge in search of food or denning sites. I saw coyote tracks at various locations and two sets of fox tracks.

Some areas of the burn had opened up views of the surrounding hills with their bright green pines and beautifully contrasting black oak leaves in shades of green, yellow, and red. The only reptile I saw was a small dead rattlesnake. I also found a beautiful, pale gray band-tailed pigeon feather nestled in the ashes.

Fire

Just before I left the burn area, I found something unusual, something that at first seemed unrelated to the fire. At the base of a fallen oak was an Indian's bowl mortar, probably just as it had been left 200 or more years ago. It reminded me of a time long past when the people of this area lived more closely with the earth. Those people could have told us that we were doing wrong when we put out all the fires.

They could have told us that fire is as important to the earth and its inhabitants as are the wind, the water, and the air.

Life's Blood

They were going to build a dam. Now they're not. Later they may change their minds.

❖ ❖ ❖ ❖ ❖ ❖ ❖ ❖ ❖ ❖

Slowly I rose to the sun's warm pull and the steady push of the wind. Higher and higher I ascended. Far below, the vast blue sea stretched from horizon to horizon, in constant turmoil, crashing upon itself. Others joined me in the air and we crowded closer and closer together.

As we continued to grow in number, we were warm, but eventually we encountered a giant wedge of cold air that began to push us eastward. Soon we could see the land, and then we were above it, billowing up over its mountains.

We grew darker and denser, colder and heavier, until the air could no longer hold our weight. We fell in a torrent, like millions of tiny bombs. We crashed into the meadows and forests, refreshing and cleansing the earth.

Life's Blood

I landed in a tall pine, was bumped by a companion, and fell 200 feet to the forest floor. I was pleased to find myself once again in the company of a tree so grand. Cool, leeward shadows of such trees had held me in a frozen condition several times in the past.

Soon I was joined by more companions, and we began to move together just below the duff. Down, ever downward we traveled, surfacing in a silver rivulet, joining other currents in a pebble-bottomed brook, and finally gathering in a small creek.

Slower, ever slower, we flowed.

❖　❖　❖　❖　❖　❖　❖　❖　❖　❖

On a previous trip, I fell from the air to the earth and joined a group that flowed into a gopher hole and began to sink into the earth. We flattened into a narrow sheet that was first vertical, then horizontal, and farther on slightly inclined. Some of the spaces we filled were as narrow as a couple of feet, and some were as wide as 50 yards. At one point, I was absorbed by

a porous rock and spent a week squeezing through, all by myself, before I rejoined my companions on our journey.

Slowly, ever downward we traveled until all of a sudden we were grabbed by capillary action, pulling us upward toward the surface of the earth. Up, ever upward we rose, until we poured out of a spring at the upper edge of a small meadow.

I've done things that many do not know I have the capacity to do. Sometimes, I've been held in reserve or done simple, monotonous, repetitive things. But there have been times when I've found myself involved in exciting, dynamic processes.

Once I was caught by the roots of a redwood, mixed with minerals, rose hundreds of feet through the tree, and was ex-pelled into the air as part of the faintest of mists, not even a shadow, almost a spirit. Eventually I became part of a cloud and once again fell to the earth.

Life's Blood

Once I found myself in the core of a beautiful white flower. The flower soon shed its petals, but I remained in its heart as it grew slowly through the summer. By fall I was part of a bright red berry that early one morning caught the eye of a hungry cedar waxwing. I traveled slowly through her digestive system and then circulated through her body as part of her blood. I spent time in her strong wing muscles and in the muscles of her tiny feet.

It wasn't the first time I'd found myself inside an animal's body. Countless times I've flowed in the blood of animals, helping to relieve the discomfort of wing muscles that ache or feet that throb by delivering fresh oxygen.

The cedar waxwing and I traveled great distances together. She deposited me more than 2,000 miles from where she'd found me, and 25 years passed before I returned to the sea.

❖ ❖ ❖ ❖ ❖ ❖ ❖ ❖ ❖ ❖

My companions and I continued to flow gently and slowly in the little creek, passing through shady corridors under the friendly umbrellas of alders and bays. Here and there we rushed through a narrow spot or fell in a sheet over a smooth rock face, but mostly we flowed slowly through crystal clear pools. In places, disease organisms joined us, but as we bubbled over rocky shallows, oxygen and the sun's ultraviolet rays killed most of them.

As we meandered through a meadow, our peaceful sounds entered the dreams of an elk bull dozing nearby. At a beautiful deep pool, a man lifted me from the creek with cupped hands and drank some of my companions, but I remained on his lower lip till he brushed me off and I fell back into the deep pool.

A coyote came to the pool for a drink and I found myself hanging from his nose as he trotted off. A short way from the pool, I fell to the ground, sank into the soil, and was eventually drawn up through the roots of a scarlet larkspur. I traveled slowly through the plant as its internal valves stopped me here and moved me there. Finally I became part of the nectar in one of its flowers.

The next morning, an Allen's hummingbird zoomed up to the flower and hung suspended in midair with wings ablur. The sunlight reflected sequins of fluorescent-green from the feathers on his back and a warm reddish-gold glow from the feathers on his bib. He sucked me up with his long slender beak, and I continued on my never-ending journey.

❖ ❖ ❖ ❖ ❖ ❖ ❖ ❖ ❖ ❖

Today I find myself once again being pulled up out of the sea and drawn eastward over the familiar mountains. My companions and I billow up and form a dark, powerful thundercloud. All of a sudden, we become hail and plummet to the ground, crushing and freezing new green grass. We join a torrent of mud and debris and tumble and spill way down through a steep canyon till we reach the familiar creek at the bottom, where we begin to flow in darkness toward the beautiful deep pool. As our progress slows, disease organisms join us, but on this trip they flourish in depths that can't be reached by the cleansing rays of the sun.

Life's Blood

When I reach the deep pool, I discover that things have changed. The pool is filling up with a stagnant black ooze and the surface is now hundreds of feet above me. I become lodged in the ooze, which will imprison me for perhaps a thousand years or more.

❖ ❖ ❖ ❖ ❖ ❖ ❖ ❖ ❖ ❖ ❖

A coyote takes a drink at the edge of a new reservoir, and a man sights in on him with a rifle. The bullet punctures the coyote's left lung and speeds on to a flowerless hillside, where brilliantly colored, tiny feathers fly as the bullet rips through the body of an Allen's hummingbird.

"Damn the coyote! It's worth more dead than alive," the man mutters as he reloads his gun.

Spring Fever

Spring Fever

Because Henry W. Coe State Park is less than an hour's drive from Silicon Valley, lots of the people who come to the park are people who work with computers. Some of our park volunteers are computer experts, and they've brought modern technology deep into the backwoods of Pine Ridge. We had computers at Coe Park long before most of the other California parks, and we have knowledgeable people who keep them running and keep us up to date on the latest hardware and software. We Coe Park lovers are grateful for such electronic advantages. But, the deeper we delve into the computer world and the more time we spend there, the more we need wild places to revive our spirits.

❖ ❖ ❖ ❖ ❖ ❖ ❖ ❖ ❖ ❖

He squinted as he tried to read the words on the screen. He'd worked hard all day, and he knew it would be way past dark before he could go home. His fingers still skipped quickly over the keyboard, but he was making more and more mistakes. The breaks he took to get just one more cup of coffee seemed to be more rejuvenating than the coffee itself. He had an important proposal to prepare and he had to get it done tonight. His manager was counting on him, and this certainly wouldn't be the first Sunday evening he'd spent at work.

He paused and glanced out the window, and just as he did, a "sharpie" flew by. "What luck to look up at that moment", he mused, and his thoughts drifted back to his last trip to Coe Park. He'd seen three sharp-shinned hawks and a Cooper's that day. It was during their fall migration way back in November, and here it was spring already. Way too much time had passed since his last soul-soothing escape to the park. Hmmmmmm...

"Get to work!" he muttered as he dragged his attention back indoors. His eyes struggled to change focus from some indiscernible object beyond the window to the screen in front of his face. He fiddled with a graphic and sent the page to the printer to see what it would look like on paper.

He dozed while he waited and woke up when he realized that nothing was printing out. Sure enough, the paper tray was empty. He added some paper, got his printout, looked it over a bit, and sat down. Then he straightened his spine, focused his eyes on the screen, and resolutely began to type on.

Before long his head began to nod and his eyelids lowered. At the brink of blankout, he pulled himself back, lifted his head, and squinted at the screen. He gazed in numbed amazement as the text dissolved and rearranged itself into the image of a monarch butterfly, filling the screen with deep oranges and black, with soft shades of yellow and points of pure white. What in the world was going on? Had he pressed some weird key combination? Was he that bleary? He squeezed his eyes shut, and when he opened them the butterfly was gone. "Concentrate," he whispered to himself through clenched teeth.

With grim determination, he composed the next paragraph in his mind and began to type, but soon he drifted off again. The whiz of the hard disk brought him back as his software application

saved whatever questionable keystrokes he'd made since the last save. As the disk spun, a warm breeze blew across his face. He lifted the nearly empty coffee cup to his lips, closed his eyes, and began to smell the alluring aromas of spring wildflowers.

"Wake up," he begged his tired brain. "Huhhhmm..... Exercise? Yes! Exercise! That'll bring me back to reality." He jumped up and began to march briskly back and forth in front of the window. As his pace slackened, he glanced outside and saw a thunderstorm building and heading his way. He watched as the clouds became darker below and billowed up higher and higher into the sky. Flickers of light danced through the clouds and jagged bolts of lightning struck the earth, as thunder rumbled in the distance. He felt cool, refreshing gusts of wind as a wall of hail approached. Soon it engulfed him, marvelous in its strength, cold on his arms, stinging his face.

He pulled himself out of the reverie, shook his head to dislodge the illusions, and wearily returned to his desk. A few minutes later, when he pressed the delete key to get rid of a typo, the screen blinked a few times and blacked out. And then, all of a sudden, a large-eared, skinny-legged mouse scurried across the screen with an agile bobcat close at its heels. He pressed all kinds of F-keys, but clearly in vain, as megabytes turned into mosquito bites, floppies into poppies, DOS into moss, and his screen widened and filled the room with a panoramic vision of Coe Park. As a last resort, he hit the escape key and was instantly whisked to Miller Field.

Oh, it feels so good to be walking briskly and breathing in deeply the fresh air of the hills. Through a field of Johnny-jump-ups, sweet little wild violets, perky and golden, all facing the sun.

That's the screech of a hawk I hear. Yeah, there it is! Soaring in circles, right over my head! And here comes another one, diving straight for the first one. Wow! The first one flipped over and they've grabbed each other by the feet! Now they're locked together, flip-flopping down through the air.

Gosh! How lucky to see this! And back up they go. Hmmmm. They've got rusty red tail feathers, so they've gotta be red-tails, and this must be the time of year for flip-flopping.

I don't know why my feet felt so tired. I didn't really walk that far. They feel much better now, with the clear waters of the East Fork flowing over them. The sounds of the creek are so soothing, but this rock's getting hard.

Hmmmm, where'd I put my shoes? Oh, there they are, under that lovely valley oak with the shiny new leaves. I think I'll join them and lie down for a while. It was a little chilly out in the open, but it's nice and warm in this sheltered, grassy spot. Just a short nap and then I'll head back.

The smells of spring are so pleasant. Mmmmmmmm... I think I could sleep here for hours....

Spring Fever

When he woke up, he found himself back at his desk. He stretched and yawned and looked out the window. The sun was low on the horizon. It must be morning. Morning...

Monday morning! It was Monday morning and his proposal was still not done! What time is it? As he lifted his wrist to check the time, his manager poked her head in. "An hour and a half till the meeting, you know. But I'm sure you're just polishing things up." She gave him an encouraging smile and left.

He took a deep breath and started to work. To his amazement and delight, his thoughts and fingers began to move at incredible speed.

An hour and ten minutes later, he was done. He clicked the print button and hummed a tune as the printer went through its paces. When the printer was finished, he gathered the pages, checked them over, and dashed to the nearest copy machine to run off copies for the meeting. Back in his office, he punched holes in the margins of one of the copies, grabbed a report binder, and headed for his manager's office.

He waited patiently while she skimmed through the pages. "This looks really good," she said and flashed him a smile. As she put the pages into the binder, she exclaimed, "Oh! What an nice touch!"

"What's that?" he asked, and leaned over her shoulder.
She reopened the binder and pointed to the inside front cover.
Right in the middle, in glorious colors, was a beautiful image
of a monarch butterfly.

Life on the Pine Ridge Ranch

I lived in Henry "Harry" Coe's old ranch house for 20 years, and every now and then someone asks me what it was like. I usually say that it was cold in the winter and hot in the summer. When the wind was blowing outside, the house was drafty and sometimes even breezy inside. When the wind blew really hard, the whole house shook and creaked like a ship in a storm. The old place seemed to be slowly sinking into the earth, from its outside edges in. A walk from the living room to one of the outside rooms was a noticeable downhill trip. Off and on throughout the years, mischievous ghosts came to visit. The windows in the house were interesting, too. I lived there for years before I realized that no two windows were the same size. No wonder sets of curtains never seemed to work out quite right. My home for those 20 years was a single-wall constructed, mudsill-set-on, sometimes haunted, antiquated old abode.

Living in the old ranch house, in the shadow of the Coe family, has been one of the most enjoyable experiences of my life. But I am now living in a spacious new "manufactured" house with central heating, insulated walls, more than sufficient *closet space, a magnificent view, earthquake bracing, and lots more. I miss the old ranch house, but time moves on and time always brings change. Work is being done to fix up the old place, and someday it will be opened to the public, at least in part, so that people for generations to come can walk inside and imagine what it was like to live this far out in the mountains just after the turn of the century. One thing will remain the same as long as this little house stands. It will always hold the memories of an earlier time when life was simple, life was hard, and life was good.*

❖ ❖ ❖ ❖ ❖ ❖ ❖ ❖ ❖ ❖

It was still dark when Harry woke up, but he knew that dawn was not far off as the rooster had already announced its near arrival. When his feet touched the cold floor, a shiver went up his shoulders and neck. He had to find his clothes in the dark, but his path from the bedroom to the living room was dimly lit by the orange glow of the few remaining coals in the fireplace. He moved the screen aside, pushed the live coals together, and stacked three logs on top. At least the living room would be warm by the time the rest of the family got up.

Harry dressed in front of the fire and went to the front door to put on his cold, stiff boots and his Levi jacket. The jacket wouldn't keep him warm, but the morning's work soon would. First to the barn to milk the cow and feed the horses. With that done, he carried an armload of small pieces of split oak from the woodshed to the cookhouse, which was attached to the main house by a narrow porch. The woodshed was less than a quarter full, which meant that warmer days were on their way and that days of pulling and pushing the double buck and swinging the double bit lay ahead.

Harry started a fire in the cook-stove. Then he went to the chicken coop, fed the chickens, and collected a half dozen eggs. "Not bad for the cool days we've been having," he said to himself. One old white leghorn hen had not been laying for several weeks. Chicken stew would be on the menu soon. He got a three-pound slab of salt pork from the cooler shed, carried the eggs and the pork to the cookhouse, and left them there for Rhoda, who was just getting out of bed.

Rhoda put on her heavy robe and lit the kerosene lantern she kept next to the bed. She carried the lantern into the living room, set it on the mantel, and sat down in the old rocking chair to put on her slippers. As she opened the front door, she paused for a moment to gaze at the pink glow of dawn silhouetting the distant mountains to the east, and then she hurried through the cold to the cookhouse. The fire Harry had started in the stove was going well and had cut the chill in the drafty little building. She felt warm and cozy, even though the cold breezes slipping into the cookhouse cooled her bare ankles.

Two cups of flour, a large pinch of salt, two teaspoons of baking powder, a quarter cup of bacon drippings, and a cup of homemade buttermilk.

Even though Rhoda made lots of buttermilk, cheese, and butter, their milk cow always produced more milk than she could use, and she often gave the extra milk to the dog, the cats, and even the calves.

Thirty stirs with the fork, twelve heaping spoonfuls into the biscuit pan, a little taste with the finger. Perfect. She wrapped a towel around the oven door handle, pulled the door open, slid the biscuit pan into the oven, and gently closed the door. After she rearranged the coals in the firebox to adjust the heat of the stove, she began to cut bacon strips from the slab of salt pork and lay them in the big cast-iron frying pan.

Harry had made a trade with Preston Thomas—butter and milk for a young pig. They kept the dressed pig hung in the cooler shed overnight and wrapped a blanket around it during the day to keep the cold in and the flies away; it would last for a few weeks that way.

Rhoda turned the handle on the coffee grinder, and as the smell ascended to her nose, she closed her eyes and took in a deep whiff. It was a smell of the morning, a smell she never grew tired of. When she measured the grounds into the coffee pot and gave them a quick stir, she enjoyed that smell too, almost as much as she would enjoy drinking a cup of coffee on this cool morning.

She removed the crisp bacon from the frying pan and poured some of the drippings into the metal cup she kept on the warming shelf of the stove just for that purpose. She set the frying pan back on the stove in a slightly cooler spot, broke two fresh eggs into the pan, and slipped the empty eggshells into the coffee pot to settle the grounds. If she hadn't cooked eggs that morning, she would have settled the grounds by pouring a little cold water around the inside edge of the pot.

As the rays of the rising sun, shining through the eastern window, projected orange images on the cookhouse walls, Rhoda pulled the pan of perfectly browned biscuits out of the oven.

Life on the Pine Ridge Ranch

Henry and Sada slept through the rooster crowing and Mom and Dad getting up, but the smell of bacon and biscuits drifting into the house brought them out of their dreams. They were up, dressed, and sitting at the table when Rhoda carried in their steaming hot breakfast plates. She set the plates on the table and headed back out to the cookhouse. Sada carefully sliced a hot biscuit open and began to spread butter on the bottom half. Henry tore open both of his biscuits and told his sister to hurry up and pass the butter. Harry and Rhoda came in, each holding a warm breakfast plate. Rhoda took the plates and set them on the table, as Harry took off his coat and hung it by the door. Before Rhoda sat down, she got a jar of sweet apricot jam from the kitchen cupboard and handed it to Sada. Rhoda had made the jam last summer with apricots picked from their orchard just west of the house. She'd also canned quince jam, applesauce, and jelly made from wild elderberries and gooseberries the kids had collected.

After breakfast, Rhoda made peanut butter sandwiches for the kids while they searched through the cooler shed for some snacks to add to their lunches. They each grabbed a tart apple from a barrel in the corner, apples picked last fall from the orchard near the abandoned Arnold homestead. Henry grabbed a handful of dried apricots from one jar and some venison jerky from another. After all, his father was always saying that he was a growing boy. Sada found two apples that were starting to spoil and put them in her pockets to save for the horses. She'd been taught that one bad apple can spoil the whole barrel.

The kids got their lunch sacks from Rhoda and saddled their horses for the 20-minute ride to the other side of Madrone Soda Springs Canyon. They could see the school, less than a half mile away, but the canyon was too steep to cross, so they'd have to go around to the Hogsback and down Cordoza Ridge until they came to the little one-room school-house on Schoolhouse Ridge. Sada fed each horse an apple and gave her father a kiss good-bye. She and Henry climbed on their horses and headed out at a walk, each knowing that

HEMEON

when they reached the spot where they could look down and see San Jose, they'd break into a gallop and race each other to school. Even though Sada was five years younger, she often beat her brother when they raced. She loved to ride, and her big sorrel quarter horse could handle the steep and rugged terrain as well as any other horse in the hills. She especially loved to help her father gather cattle on horseback.

With the kids off to school, Rhoda got dressed, finished washing the dishes, and started to wash clothes. Her stove didn't have a hot water heater, so she heated water on top of the stove in a large copper washtub. Since it was still cold outside, she did the laundry inside the cookhouse. If it had been summer, she would have carried the tub and scrub board outside to wash clothes. She loved basking in the warmth of the summer sun, but she certainly didn't miss cooking and working around the stove on hot summer days.

Life on the Pine Ridge Ranch

Harry grabbed his lunch, gave Rhoda a hug, and mounted his horse. This morning he headed for Blue Ridge, leading a pack-horse loaded down with rock salt and tools. Today was the day he'd set aside for fixing the spring box and trough at Tule Spring and for putting rock salt out for the cattle. He would put the salt in boxes and set the boxes in areas where his cattle hadn't recently grazed. He also planned to spend several hours moving the cattle around with the help of Bruce, his cattle dog. He didn't really need to move the cattle (the rock salt would eventually accomplish that), but he liked to work cattle with his horse, and it would keep the cattle from becoming wild and skittish around people and dogs.

❖ ❖ ❖ ❖ ❖ ❖ ❖ ❖ ❖ ❖ ❖

Harry found himself returning through the Arnold Field as the sun neared the western horizon. He stretched out a tired arm and used his fingers to measure the distance between the horizon and the sun. Two fingers; he still had 30 minutes before the sun set. Time enough to get back, unsaddle, and unload the horses before dark. The kids would have their chores done and dinner would be on the table by the time he finished washing up, using Rhoda's homemade soap and the water pitcher and bowl he'd packed all the way from the East when he brought his new bride to California.

As he approached the large, lone pine near the edge of the Arnold field, he stopped to relax for a moment and reflect on the day. With his arms crossed on top of the saddle horn, he looked to the west, toward his home. The colors of a magnificent sunset spread across the land and the sky, and he could just pick out the outline of his little ranch house, nestled among the silhouetted oaks and pines. He'd done some hard work today, but he'd also taken time to enjoy the beauty of the early wildflowers, the gorgeous views from the ridge tops, and the freshness of the briskly flowing streams. Life was simple, life was hard, and life was good.

Life in an Oak Tree

I was surrounded by oak trees in the East Bay suburb where I grew up. When I've lived away from oaks, I've missed them and have sought them out on my days off. Now, at Coe Park, I'm surrounded by oak trees again, and the better I get to know them, the more marvelous I find them to be. All oaks are wonderful, but my favorites are the black oaks and the valley oaks.

❖ ❖ ❖ ❖ ❖ ❖ ❖ ❖ ❖ ❖

From a distance you could see a swing beneath the spreading branches of the huge valley oak. It was just an old tire hung by a rope to one of the tree's massive limbs. You had to get a bit closer to see the tree house perched between three large branches about twenty feet above the ground. We built the tree house out of spare wood Dad gave us and with scraps of plywood from the houses they were building in the vacant lots across the road. Although we often spent the night in the tree house, we usually didn't sleep much. In the flickering candle-light, the hooting of the great horned owls and the cries of the mourning doves seemed more like the sounds that terrible monsters might make.

Life in an Oak Tree

People could live in trees, I suppose, but there are thousands
of plants and animals that are much better suited to life in
an oak. An oak tree is like a whole world unto itself. For some
organisms, the entire cycle of birth, life, and death takes place
on a single tree. The tree provides water, oxygen, shelter from
the elements, protection from predators, and nourishment in
many forms — in essence, everything an organism might need
throughout its life.

An oak tree's shade and the moisture around it provide an
ideal habitat for simple forms of life. All surfaces on an oak
tree and the ground beneath it are home to mosses, lichens,
and fungi.

If you want to see mosses in their prime, take a walk through
an oak forest or woodland during the winter. When the mosses
are lush and bright green from the winter rains, it's hard to
resist running your fingers over their soft leaves. People who
are lost in the woods can use moss as a compass. Mosses
really do grow primarily on the north side of trees. On the
north side, they're protected from the sun and they have the
moisture that's essential to their growth.

There are three kinds of lichen: crustose, foliose, and fruti-
cose, and all three kinds live on oaks. Their names are based
on the way they look. Crustose lichens form a low crusty
growth, and though they do grow on trees, they're more
commonly found on rocks. Foliose lichens have a leafy appear-
ance, like the foliage of plants. Fruticose lichens have stringy,
sometimes interwoven strands of growth that give them a
bushy look. You might expect that fruticose lichens would be
shaped like cherries or pears, but the word fruticose actually
comes from the Latin word for shrub.

Lichens are actually two kinds of organisms in one, a fungus
and an alga that live in a mutually beneficial alliance. The
fungus is the structure that we see; it provides the alga with
a place to live, with minerals, and with the moisture that is
essential to life for the water-loving alga. In return, the alga

Coast Live Oak

provide food for the fungus. Algae harness the sun's energy and manufacture the carbohydrates that the fungus cannot live without.

Lace lichen and old man's beard are two of the more conspicuous lichens that grow on California oaks. Both are fruticose lichens, and both have grayish-green strands that drape over tree limbs. They look a lot like the Spanish moss that grows in southern states, but Spanish moss is neither a lichen nor a moss. It's a bromeliad, a relative of the pineapple.

Mushrooms are found in all oak forests and woodlands. They have a network of rootlike structures called mycelium that permeate living and dead plant material and absorb nutrients. The tasty morsels we buy in the grocery store are called mushrooms, but they're only the reproductive part of the mushroom fungus. The rest of the fungus is hidden from sight, spreading sometimes for many feet through organic material.

Mushrooms, other fungi, and bacteria are solely responsible for the decay and decomposition of all organic matter, and they can be found wherever other forms of life exist. They recycle organic material by breaking it down into the basic ingredients required for new life.

Mushrooms and oak trees live in close association. As an oak gets old and weak, some mushroom species invade the tree, absorbing its essential nutrients, decomposing its tissues, and speeding its death. Other mushroom species form a mutually beneficial alliance with oak trees, a commingling that biologists call a mycorrhizal relationship.

Life in an Oak Tree

The mushroom's mycelium penetrate the roots of an oak and supply it with nitrogen, phosphorus, and other nutrients that the tree cannot easily obtain on its own. The roots of the tree give the mushroom the moisture and organic compounds essential to its survival.

Insects by far outnumber all other organisms that rely on oak trees. One group of insects, the oak gall wasps, cannot exist without oaks. More than 200 species of oak gall wasps live in California, and each species deposits its eggs in the tissues of an oak tree. Different species select different parts of a tree, and you can find their galls all over the tree—on the bark, leaves, stems, roots, and acorns. The eggs hatch into wormlike larvae, and the larvae excrete chemicals that cause the tree to produce a tumorlike growth—the gall. The gall encloses the larvae and provides them with food and shelter until they're ready to bore their way through to the world outside. Species other than gall wasps make use of galls and the larvae inside them. Some insect species feed on the galls, others eat the larvae, and some are larval parasites.

STEM GALL

OAK APPLE GALL

BLUE OAK LEAF GALL

Galls come in a dazzling assortment of shapes, colors, and sizes. Some are as large as baseballs, and some are so small that you may never notice them. Blue oaks have the showiest galls. They also have the greatest variety; a single blue oak tree can have over 20 different kinds of galls on it. For example, on a blue oak leaf you can find several kinds of pink to dark red galls, all pea-sized or slightly larger. One resembles a fuzzy little ball, one looks like a thorny red crown, and another one resembles a sea urchin.

If you think you've seen an apple growing on the stem of a valley oak tree, what you've probably discovered is a gall called an oak apple. It's a smooth, round gall that changes in color as it matures, from green to pink to gray to black. Hikers often come across oak apple galls lying on the ground. Some know that they've found a gall, but others may still be puzzled about those mysterious round objects.

Many species of birds live in oak forests and woodlands and nest within the protective foliage of the trees. Woodpeckers, nuthatches, and warblers thrive on the insects that live in oak trees, and they exist in harmony with each other because they eat different kinds of insects and collect them from different parts of the tree.

Life in an Oak Tree

The stealthy Cooper's hawk is attracted to oak woodlands because of the other birds that live there. Cooper's hawks often nest in oaks, and you may spot one darting and gliding swiftly through the boughs of the trees, hunting for smaller birds to eat.

Valley Oak

Acorns play a vital role in the natural history of California. Because of their abundance, high nutritional value, and availability during the winter months, they are considered the most important source of food for California wildlife. Many animals feed on acorns, and those that do are preyed upon by other animals.

Oak trees and animals can sometimes form interesting partnerships. Squirrels and acorn-loving birds like the scrub jay gather acorns and store them in the ground so that they can rely on them as food later in the year when they can't find much else to eat. A single scrub jay may bury several thousand acorns during the fall. The jay will dig up and eat many of the acorns in the winter, but it never finds them all. Some of the overlooked acorns, so conveniently planted, grow into new oak trees.

Blue Oak

The acorn-storing animals thrive on the meat of the acorns, and the oak trees get a free distribution service.

Life in an Oak Tree

Western Scrub Jay

Early in California history, naturalists wondered how oak trees could end up on the sides and tops of our rolling hills and steep ridges since acorns obviously can't roll uphill. When the naturalists discovered the acorn-stashing habits of jays and squirrels, the mystery was solved.

The most notorious acorn-eating birds are the acorn wood-peckers. These noisy little clown-face birds live in communal groups, and they make sure that they always have an ample supply of acorns. They drill holes in trees and stuff the holes with acorns, moving the acorns to smaller holes as the acorns dry out and shrink in size. When a woodpecker is hungry for an acorn, it cracks one open and eats the acorn meat, along with any insect larvae it finds inside. The trees where the woodpeckers store their acorns are called granaries, and a single tree may have as many as 10,000 acorn-stuffed holes.

The sapsucker is a seldom-seen woodpecker. What you're more likely to see are the sets of horizontal holes sapsuckers drill in the trunks of oaks and other trees to reach the sap-producing layers inside. Although sapsuckers eat a fair amount of tree sap, insects make up a larger part of their diet.

Mistletoe sucks much more sap from oak trees than the sapsuckers do, but it depends on birds for its successful propagation. Oak mistletoe berries are eaten by jays, western bluebirds, cedar waxwings, and other berry-loving birds. As the berries pass through the digestive tract of a bird, their seeds become capable of germinating. If a bird deposits a seed on the limb of an oak, in just the right sort of spot,

Life in an Oak Tree

the seed develops rootlike structures that bore into the oak. As the mistletoe grows, it absorbs water and minerals from an oak, but it doesn't rely entirely on the tree for its sustenance. Oak mistletoe is a green plant, and like all green plants it can produce its own food. An oak tree may be stressed by an abundance of mistletoe, and some limbs may have dead zones beyond thick mistletoe growths, but the plant doesn't kill healthy trees. As an oak gets old and weak, it is more susceptible to damage from fungi, insects, and mistletoe, all of which can be contributing factors to its death.

Mammals are common in oak woodlands, and they sometimes make an oak tree their home. A hollow trunk with an opening near the ground is likely to be claimed by a skunk, fox, bobcat, ground squirrel, or wood rat, depending on the size of the hole, and a raccoon will take up residence in a hollow area if the opening is farther up the tree.

Deer are more dependent on oaks than any other mammal. The adults and fawns eat lots of acorns during the fall. The oil-rich acorns help fawns put on the fat they may need to make it through a harsh winter. If the grown deer have plenty of acorns to eat in the fall, they'll be more fertile in the spring, and the does will have a better chance of giving birth to twins.

Deer also eat the leaves and twigs of oak trees. In open areas, you're likely to see a browse line at the base of oak foliage that shows how high the deer can reach. By wintertime, when the deciduous oaks have lost their leaves, deer turn to two of their favorite browse foods—the lichens and mistletoe that cling to the oaks.

Acorns were the most important source of food for the Native Americans who lived in our area. Their populations were relatively small until they discovered that acorns could be used for food.

Raw acorns are essentially inedible; eating one would be as unpleasant as eating an olive right off the tree. Long ago, some incredibly clever or particularly patient person found that you can remove the bitter tannin from mashed acorns by repeatedly pouring water over them. Suddenly there was a massive new food crop available to Native Americans, since about 30 percent of the land in California was covered with oak forests or woodlands.

When the Native Americans in California adopted oaks as their staple crop, they no longer had to wander over large areas hunting for animals. Acorns gave them a protein-rich, carbohydrate-filled, tasty food that was easy to gather, easy to store, and relatively easy to prepare. Their populations soared. The mortar holes found throughout California are testimony to the value of the acorn.

❖ ❖ ❖ ❖ ❖ ❖ ❖

From our tree house, we could see lots of oak trees and just a few houses. But that would change. One summer evening we heard the growl of a chain saw off in the distance. A few days later, while we were exploring the far side of the new housing development, we found a big valley oak tree lying on the ground. We didn't know why it had been cut down. Maybe someone wanted to use it for firewood, or maybe they wanted to make room for a road or another house.

We spent the whole afternoon climbing all over the tree, finding many wonderful things and having a glorious time. Still, I couldn't get over the feeling that something wasn't quite right. It made me sad to see the huge tree lying broken on the ground. Before we left, we counted its rings. The tree was over 500 years old that summer, and I had just turned twelve.

Something Stinks in Here

I enjoy writing stories that well up from the depths of my imagination, but as the old saying goes, "Truth is stranger than fiction," and ain't it the truth. The events described in this story really happened, and besides, it would be hard to spin a yarn as far-fetched and fragrant.

❖ ❖ ❖ ❖ ❖ ❖ ❖ ❖ ❖ ❖

On your first day of work at a park with pit toilets, you can be sure that you'll be expected to learn the fine art of cleaning them. I got toilet trained on my first day as a Mt. Diablo park aid, and so did Dede Villareal on her first day as a park aid at Coe Park. Dede's training was a little more complicated than mine though, as things turned out.

To digress for a moment, ever since I started in parks, I've wondered why we call those little wooden enclosures "pit toilets." "Outhouse" isn't a very inviting name either, but it beats the heck out of pit toilet. When I think of a pit, I think of something you catch wild animals in.

Something Stinks in Here

Getting back to the story, John Neef, the Coe Park maintenance worker, took Dede down to the campground on her first day of training to teach her how to deal with pit toilets. After he cleaned the first two, he handed Dede the bucket and said, "The next four are all yours." Full of first-day spunk, she cheerfully went to work, even though the atmosphere of the work in question doesn't normally lend itself to cheer.

People who've dealt with pit toilets are familiar with a certain smell, a particular aroma, shall we say, that hovers around pit toilets and nowhere else. All pit toilets have that distinctive smell, every single one, and nothing else smells quite the same. I think that Dede must have learned this law of nature as she cleaned her first three pit toilets, because a few moments after she entered number four, she was heard to say, "Something stinks in here!"

That remark would probably not have seemed unreasonable to the casual walker-by, but Dede had outdoors experience. The stink she referred to in the fourth pit toilet was one she was familiar with; it was the odor of skunk. She carefully bent over and looked behind the commode, thinking the skunk was probably hiding back there. To her surprise... no skunk. Where else could it be? Only one other place to look... in the pit. She looked, and sure enough, the skunk was sleeping down below. The first problem was solved; Dede had determined the location of the skunk. The next problem was a little trickier... how to get it out. Things could have been worse, though, if someone had tried to use the toilet after the skunk took up residence.

This situation was obviously too much for a first-day park aid, so Dede went and found John. John decided the problem called for a committee, so he went and found me. John made a crude sign that said, "Stay Away, Skunk in Toilet," tacked it to the toilet door, and stepped back looking like he'd certainly done his part. I located a long two-by-four and suggested that Dede lower it into the pit. She did, and then we all stood back and waited, hoping against hope that the skunk would scramble up and make its getaway. No such luck.

66

Next, John fashioned a rather impressive looking "skunk ladder" and lowered it into the pit. Even though skunks normally sleep during the day and they must be able to tolerate pretty strong smells, I was fairly confident that the animal would soon get tired of its accommodations and scramble up the ladder. But skunk noses must be much weaker than I thought; several hours passed, and the beast was still down there.

Figuring that the Humane Society wouldn't get near this problem and that the wildlife rescue people would realize they were going to be tied up rescuing mosquito larva in Guatemala for the next few days, we decided to try the old rope and bucket trick. With the rope strung through a loop in the toilet ceiling, we slowly lowered the bucket into the pit. "I bet the skunk will climb right in, looking for a darker spot, like a hole in a tree," I commented cheerfully. Once again, no such luck.

Something Stinks in Here

When you make careless comments like that, you can expect to be the one volunteered to try and nudge the skunk into the bucket with the two-by-four. Although the skunk was un-cooperative, he didn't seem to be too upset about the board at first. After a few more persistent nudges, however, he must have gotten a little irritated because he raised his tail and aimed straight up. Moments later, a stinky little cloud passed in front of my nose and blew right into John, who was standing in the doorway. The toilet was temporarily abandoned.

We gave the animal a few minutes to calm down and went back to work. I gave him a couple of determined shoves with the board and he crawled into the bucket. "It's in!" I hollered as I dashed out the door, while John and Dede took off with the rope. Our fleeing figures were closely followed by a large yellow cloud.

Mission accomplished. The skunk was free, but was sure to be barred from the den for a while. The rescuers were allowed back in their homes, but they immediately had to strip off their clothes and hop in the tub.

Let's see now... isn't there some kind of moral to this story?

... Nah

Pronghorn

In early March of 1990, for just a few days, three pronghorn were seen in the Arnold Field and nearby areas. The sightings created a lot of excitement at Coe Park, and we got on the phone to find out where they'd come from. Before long, we learned that the California Department of Fish and Game had released a group of pronghorn on the neighboring Hewlett-Packard property.

❖ ❖ ❖ ❖ ❖ ❖ ❖ ❖ ❖ ❖

They ran from the sweathouse, but this time they did not jump into the cool water of the nearby stream. This time they wanted to keep their scent concealed by the lingering smell of smoke from the sweathouse fire. One of them, a slender young man, knew pronghorn would be wandering into the valley any day, as they did every year at this time. But this year would be special for him. This year he would hunt them for the first time.

He jogged two miles from his isolated canyon village to a dirt bench on a bluff that sat about 24 feet above the wide part of the valley, with a northwestern exposure. He squatted on the bench, focused his attention inward, and sat perfectly still, with his bow and arrow ready. He felt the warmth of the morning's sun as it projected itself through the blue oaks in moving, mosaic patterns on his back. He didn't have a word for photosynthesis, but he knew that the leaves of the trees were absorbing the energy of the sun, and he knew that the same energy would drive the swift legs of his adversary. He hoped that he would do well this day, but he felt something stronger than hope. He felt deep in his spirit that the time was right, and that the circle would soon be completed.

With his eyes half closed, he remembered the autumn when his grandfather had taken him on a journey to the great valley in the east. He had been a young boy then, and the trip had been hard for him, but he would never forget the joy he had felt when he and his grandfather crested the last ridge. The evening sun was setting, casting long shadows across the lowlands and lighting up the beautiful foothills and magnificent mountains beyond the valley. He and his grandfather had watched silently as thousands of pronghorns moved throughout the valley, grazing on the abundant grasses and wildflowers.

He remained alert, but he let part of his mind continue to wander through years gone by as he recalled his previous encounters with pronghorns and contemplated his admiration for their grace and beauty.

He'd been squatting practically motionlessly for almost two hours when all of a sudden a herd of about 36 pronghorn came running up through the valley toward him. As the animals drew nearer, a shiver of anticipation ran through his body, but he gathered his concentration and held himself still.

He felt something on his left ankle, glanced down, and saw a large red ant crawling up his leg. It just tickled a little, moving through the hairs on his calf, but he knew that if it bit, he might not be able to remain still. With a graceful movement of his arm, carefully matching the rhythm of the swaying oak branches nearby, he gently flicked the ant to the ground.

The pronghorn slowed as they reached the wider part of the valley, and he watched intently as they began to spread out and feed on buckwheat, goldenbush, and other low shrubs. He slowly raised his bow, but not to shoot. Attached to one end of the bow was the feather of a golden eagle, and it began to twist and flutter in the breeze. He knew that pronghorn are curious by nature, so he held the bow steady and waited.

Pronghorn

A good-sized doe caught sight of the feather and began to move in his direction to investigate. Not all the does had horns, but this one did. Her horns were short spikes, about a third the length of an arrow. All the full grown bucks had horns. Their horns had two prongs, and some were more than half the length of an arrow.

As the pronghorn approached, he began to focus on her beauty. Her coat was a striking contrast of two colors. Her back, shoulders, and legs were covered with rich tan fur. Soft white fur covered her rump, ran under her belly and up the front of her neck, where two tan bars crossed it.

She had large, brown, protruding eyes that were set far back on the sides of her head. With those eyes she could see far, as far as an eagle can see, and she could see much; without moving her head, she had an almost 360-degree field of view. Her eyes and her vigilance protected her well from coyote, wolf, and mountain lion.

Her dark black nose, covered with a shiny wet film, twitched as she sniffed the air for clues about the fluttering object up on the bluff. She cautiously moved closer. When she was about 20 feet from him, he thought, "Should I shoot now? Should I wait?"

His mind flashed back to the year before. He and his father had been waiting at the same spot, silently watching while a wary buck approached. Just as his father took aim and shot, the buck stepped on a dry twig. The twig snapped, the buck bolted, and the arrow struck the ground. Nearby pronghorn were alarmed. Their white rump patches nearly doubled in size as they flashed a warning signal. The signal was quickly picked up and passed along, and the whole herd took off. Within moments they were far away, their images obscured in a haze of dust.

As the memory faded, he began to worry. "What if I miss? What if I just wound her? What if...? ..Stop thinking! Trust your instincts as you were taught." He relaxed and felt the circle closing. He knew it was time. He quickly lowered his loaded bow, pulled back, and released the arrow. And with the arrow he released an inner power that sent the arrow straight to the animal's heart. She turned, then dropped. She had given her life for him. They were both a part of the whole. In respect for her, he would waste nothing.

She weighed about 100 pounds, and he didn't have an easy time with her, but he soon got her hoisted over his shoulders and began the two-mile trip home. He felt a sense of pride and jubilation as he approached the village. When his people saw him, they ran to him and welcomed him with expressions of appreciation and congratulations. He basked in the warmth of their emotions for a little while, but then he took the pronghorn to his hut and began the process he had learned from his father and grandfather. He began to dress the animal out.

Her meat would be shared by the whole tribe. Her tendons would be used to attach arrowheads to arrow shafts. Her slender leg bones would be highly prized for their strength. Her legs had to be strong, strong enough to go 50 miles an hours to outrun coyotes and wolves, strong enough to burst into speeds of up to 70 miles an hour to escape the pounce and swift pursuit of mountain lions. Her leg bones would be used to make strong awls and other tools.

The most valuable prize of all was her pelt. It had served her well, the fine insulating properties of the tubular hairs keeping her warm in the winter and cool in the summer. It would serve him well too. The pronghorn could raise its own hairs to help ventilate its body, but he would have to brush the hair to keep it raised. The horns, with their little prongs, would serve many purposes. These horns were actually antlers that pronghorn shed each year, but unlike the antlers of deer and elk, the pronghorn's antlers attach to true horns that are permanent.

Soon many changes would come about. White men would hunt the pronghorn until they were nearly gone. The pronghorn, often mistakenly called antelope (their unusual horns put them in a group separate from the true antelope), numbered over

Pronghorn

40 million before the coming of the Europeans. At the beginning of the 19th century, their numbers had been reduced to less than 20 thousand. They were killed by the thousands by market hunters for food, by trappers for hides, and, sadly, by others just for the fun of it.

A man knelt on a low bench 20 feet above the wide part of a valley. He knew that a horse or a vehicle could not catch the speedy pronghorn, but a dangling feather would bring them close enough to shoot. A good sized doe approached to within 50 feet. The magazine was loaded, and he knew he would not miss as he sighted on the doe.

He took aim at the beautiful animal and slowly squeezed — click. Then more clicks. He got off five shots before the herd bolted and in seconds they were beyond the range of his camera. He smiled. He felt the circle close. The pronghorn that had been near extinction had grown back to over 400,000 and were being introduced into areas they had been gone from for more than 100 years.

The Monument Pine

Soon after I moved to Coe Park, I began to meet particularly interesting trees and to call them by their given names. My kids named Sada's Pine, I named the octopus tree, someone had named the corkscrew tree, everyone agreed on the name of the rattlesnake tree (after personal experiences), and Bob Patrie had named the Monument Pine. The huge tree grew near the monument, and the tree itself was truly monumental.

The Monument Pine

You could see it from any high place in the park and from many places outside the park, including the Santa Clara Valley. It was undoubtedly the largest and oldest Ponderosa Pine living in Coe Park.

❖ ❖ ❖ ❖ ❖ ❖ ❖ ❖ ❖ ❖ ❖

Darkness covered the ridge top. A strong wind blew through the pines as the rain soaked the earth. A ray of light reached a tiny seed buried only inches deep in the duff, and I was born! My roots began to grow to the pull of gravity, and against that power my body rose slowly into the air. Within a few weeks my little branches had green needles and I was independent of the nurturing influences of my parents, except for the summer shade and winter wind protection they continued to give me in my early years.

Life was difficult as I grew up. Every spring the deer chewed on my tender young branches. One winter, before I was two feet tall, I was covered with snow for a week. Many of my siblings were consumed by deer and rodents, and others died when they were bent over and broken by the snow. (When I was much older, a particularly hard snow one year broke my top off, but I was mature enough to withstand the damage.)

I was almost eight feet tall when a fire swept over the ridge and destroyed all my lower limbs. I survived, but I grew very slowly for a while. Then, during the following winter, the nutrients released by the fire soaked into the earth, and with bright new, shiny-green needles, I began to grow faster than ever before. Another fire came through when I was almost 20 feet tall, and again my lower limbs were burned. But afterwards, even though fires continued to burn across the ridge top every few years, my lowest limbs were out of the reach of the flames, and fire would hurt me no more.

Insects crawled all over me, some even attacked, but I was strong and had many allies. In particular, the birds were great friends. The nuthatches spent the summer months picking insects from under my bark. Their friendly little honking call was one of my favorite sounds; I was grateful when they used me as their home. There were lots of acorn woodpeckers, too. They also helped keep insects down, but they did insist upon drilling holes into my bark and filling them with acorns. Even so, I considered them friends because they did little true damage, and I enjoyed their antics, and their comical looks. I didn't mind the droppings left by the birds. When winter came, I would be washed and blown clean by the storms.

There were years when the rain was light and the cleansing power was weak. During those years, there was little to drink, but I had set deep roots and I survived. Other, even older trees became weak (as any living thing does without water) and the attacking insects eventually killed some of them.

As I grew up, people would come by. For many years they paid little attention to me, although they did collect and eat my seeds, like many other animals did. As I grew very tall, some people would gaze at me for long stretches of time, revering nature's work. That made me feel good.

As I became quite old, others came and cut down some of the trees, even some of my own offspring, and used them to build their homes. Then, in 1952, a special woman, one who had often stared up through my branches with reverence, decided as she sat against my trunk, that she would protect this land for all time. No more cattle to eat our offspring, no more bulldozers to dig them up, no more saws to take the strongest in their prime.

The Monument Pine

My life had been wonderfully long and full. I knew of none older. On December 15, 1988, a strong wind from out of the east snapped me off at my base and I fell to the earth. A ray of light shined through my prostrate branches and touched a tiny seed, a ray of light that is part of me.

Farewell to the Monument Pine,
a guiding point while alive.
Let us continue to learn from you,
the lessons we need to survive.

Sometimes Things Just Fall into Place

I've seen more than 20 mountain lions in the wild, which is considerably more than a lucky person could expect to see in a lifetime. Mountain lions are my favorite animal, by far, and I consider the sightings I've had as unique blessings. The Rick I refer to in this story is now Dr. Rick Hopkins. We first met a few weeks after I arrived at Coe Park in 1977. He was at that time just starting his mountain lion research in the Diablo Range. He studied lions in the area for the next 12 years, earning first his Masters degree in Biology and then his Ph.D in Wildlands Resource Science. This is a true story about my favorite mountain lion sighting (so far).

Sometimes Things Just Fall into Place

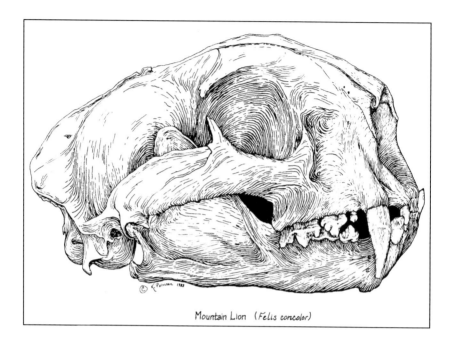

Mountain Lion (*Felis concolor*)

Sometimes, when things seem to be falling apart,
they're really just falling back into place.

It was Thursday, my birthday, and on Saturday I was scheduled
to give a program on mountain lions at Sunol Regional Wilder-
ness. The program was initially to be given at Coe Park, but the
road to the park had slid out, leaving a large impassible area
where the Calaveras earthquake fault parallels East Dunne
Avenue. The unstable area was not going to be repaired for
a few more months, so the location of my program was moved
to Sunol.

As I was leaving Coe Park, on rough backcountry roads, I was
thinking about my program's introduction, which included my
close encounter with a female lion and her cub just a few weeks
after I arrived at the park in 1977.

With lions foremost in my mind, seeing what appeared to be
an African lion in the road ahead didn't seem too far out of line.

Sometimes Things Just Fall into Place

"Surely just a deer," I said to myself. When I got nearer, I was delighted to see that my African lion was actually an adult female mountain lion with a cub. As I got close to them, the cub ran towards and past my jeep, and I saw it plop down in the grass in an open field. I stopped and watched. The cub's mother, wearing one of Rick's lion-study collars, walked up on a hill just 20 feet from me.

I quietly got out of the jeep and began to follow the mother lion for a short distance but stopped short when she turned her head toward me and growled. My urge to get closer to this animal, in my mind the strongest, most beautiful, and most graceful animal of the park, was quickly diminished by her meaningful growl. She walked across a swale and stood 100 feet away on a knoll in the shadow of a blue oak, barely visibly now. If I hadn't known she was there under the tree, I could have walked to within 20 feet of the tree without noticing her.

I remembered the cub and walked toward the spot where it had plopped down, thinking it would undoubtedly be gone by now. I kept an eye on mom, still only 100 feet away. I knew it was foolhardy to go searching for a lion cub when its mother was less that 20 bounds and 5 seconds away, but I simply didn't feel any fear. I walked to where I thought I'd seen the cub lie down, but it wasn't there. Surely it had gone. This was wide open grassland and I could see all around. "Maybe it's just a little more to my right," I thought to myself.

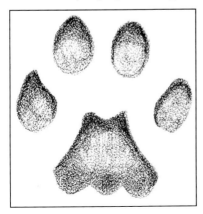

A slightly different color caught my eye about ten feet away. "Just some rocks," I figured.

When I got to within six feet of "the rocks," I clearly saw a small, spotted mountain lion cub staring at me! Absolutely the cutest little thing I'd seen since I first laid eyes on my newborn daughter.

Sometimes Things Just Fall into Place

The cub decided I was too close and ran quickly to the east, instinctively toward mom.

As I headed to town, my spirits were soaring. I'd just had the most thrilling lion encounter of my life, and I began thinking about how I'd use the story in my program. Gone was the discontentment of a fallen road, having to live in two houses at one time, and a two-hour commute over rough roads.

When I arrived at our temporary "summer house" Quonset hut, my daughter had a special birthday gift for me, a lovely little porcelain figurine of a baby mountain lion. It sits on my nightstand to this day.

Spring

I look forward to spring each year, and each year I promise myself that I'll spend more time outside during that glorious season. When the last mariposa lily has shriveled and the pink has faded from the last farewell-to-spring, I think back and realize that I ended up spending far too much time pushing papers, too much time reading, too much time in front of a computer, and too much time looking longingly out windows.

83

Spring

Spring is already coming again, and I'm getting out more than usual, but will I be able to keep it up? I certainly hope so.... Oh, I'm connected finally, and I've got mail. Forty-two messages! Well, I guess I'll just gaze out the window till they're all downloaded.

❖ ❖ ❖ ❖ ❖ ❖ ❖ ❖ ❖ ❖ ❖

Spring officially begins toward the end of March, but long before March arrives, you'll see signs of spring in the Diablo Range. In January, and maybe even as early as December,

Manzanita Blossoms

the delicate, white, bell-shaped flowers of the manzanita shrubs bloom, braving the short days and cold winds. White-flowered milkmaids begin to bloom in February, and long before most people begin thinking of spring, plump bumblebees are out feeding on the nectar of the blue forget-me-not hound's tongue flowers. It's about this time when the deciduous oak trees that for months have stood naked, seemingly life-less, and almost two-dimensional in appearance, develop red-tinted twigs with swollen buds at their tips. The trees take on a glow and a more three-dimensional appearance. In weeks or even days, they leaf out, and before long the forest is shiny, bright, and green again.

The birds that flew south to escape the short, cold days of winter begin to return to nest and raise their young, relying on the bounty of spring in Northern California. The turkey vultures, like the manzanita blossoms, arrive early. They soar over the landscape and seem totally in their element as they're buffeted about by the cold, gusty winds of late winter.

If you spend time outdoors in spring, you're bound to hear the lovely song of a sort of drab little bird. If you spot the singer, you might be surprised to discover that it's what has for years been called a plain titmouse, a bird that's spent the months since last spring just being plain. These perky, crested little forest dwellers have been aptly renamed oak titmice, and although they remain somewhat plain looking, they continue to show off their joyful

Milkmaids

(and definitely not plain) personalities as they flit from oak tree to oak tree in search of new spring bugs.

As the days get longer, they also become noticeably warmer. We still get periods of unsettled weather, but rainbows forecast the marvelous days ahead. You catch a whiff of fragrant ceanothus blossoms, and suddenly your spirits soar. Before you know it, spring is here in all its glory, and what started as a hint and built into a steady stream has all of a sudden become a flash flood of colors and sounds and smells that brighten the whole world.

Oak Titmouse

Spring

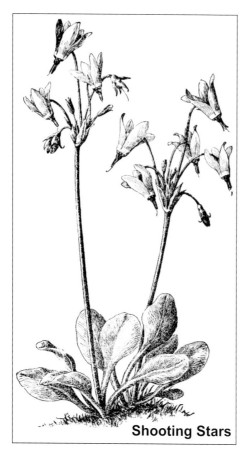

Shooting Stars

Wildflowers are one of the most precious gifts of spring, and the Diablo Range is one of the best places in the world to seek them out and enjoy them. Let me tell you a little about some of my favorites.

The lowland shooting stars with their chubby downward-facing rocket flowers are one of the earliest flowers, but their blooming time depends mostly on how early the rains come.

Some years lowland shooting stars have begun to bloom as early as December (a friend of mine woke up surrounded by a meadow full of magenta shooting stars one Christmas morning), but in years of late rains, they may not begin to bloom until late February.

The green-stemmed lowland shooting stars of open meadows fade early, but the woodland shooting stars, growing in shady locations, last well into spring. The more graceful woodland species has slender downward-facing rocket flowers so slender that the rockets are often thought to look like mosquitoes with long slender bills (and thus the other common name, mosquito bills). The woodland shooting stars also have magenta flowers but they grow above a reddish, longer stem. If shooting stars remind you of the garden cyclamens, you have a good eye for flowers. Both are in the primrose family.

My favorite wild violets are the Johnny-jump-ups. You'll find them covering large areas in many a grassy meadow, their glowing little yellow faces brightening the open grasslands. If you keep your eye on Johnny-jump-ups, you'll notice that their flowers always face the sun. You can walk out a trail towards the sun and not notice any, but when you turn around to return, there they all are, facing you and the sun.

Johnny-Jump-Up

There are two less common species of yellow violets in the park that you might mistake for Johnny-jump-ups, until you take a closer look. One species, the oak violet, grows in the shade of trees. Its petals are smaller and paler than Johnny-jump-up petals, and its leaves are longer and more gray-green in color. If you're walking through one of the drier areas of the park and you see a violet with deeper yellow flowers and finely divided leaves, you've discovered a Douglas violet.

The only other violet we have in the park is a white-flowered violet that grows along some of the creeks. It's called the two-eyed violet because the two outer petals have a dark purple spot in the middle.

Delphinium

Spring

Two-Eyed Violet

The two-eyed violet is not common in the park, and it's always a pleasure to find it growing along a shady creek bank.

You'll find several species of larkspurs throughout the park, most of them in shades of blue and purple. Larkspurs are also called delphiniums because of their genus name Delphinium, which was derived from the Greek word for dolphins. The name was chosen because the nectar "spur" flower buds resemble dolphins. My favorite larkspur is the red larkspur. It's not very common in the park, but if you're lucky, you might come across some along the East Fork of the Coyote Creek (in the narrows area) or in the canyon of the Little Fork.

Another rather uncommon flower in the park is the beautiful crimson (or red) columbine. The word columbine comes from a Latin word for dovelike. The plant grows only in moist canyons, and there's a nice patch that you can't miss along the Flat Frog Trail, if the flowers are in bloom. When you find a columbine, take a close look at one of its blossoms. If you squint your eyes and use your imagination, the five petals and their upward pointing nectar spurs look like a circle of five doves facing each other.

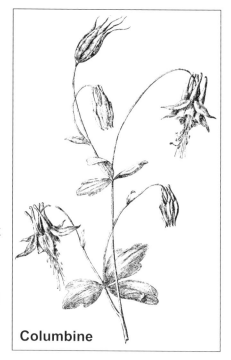

Columbine

Iris is the Greek word for rainbow, and irises do come in a rainbow of colors. We have only one species in the park, the ground iris, and its blossoms are a dreamy shade of blue. Irises belong to the Iris family (sometimes things are simple), and we have one other member of the family in the park, California blue-eyed grass. Common names are often misleading, even downright deceptive. Blue-eyed grass, for example, is not a grass, its "eye" is not blue (it's yellow), and the color of the flower is much closer to purple than it is to blue. And, if that's not confusing enough, a few unusual blue-eyed grass plants in the park have white flowers. I found one "white-eyed grass" plant near the Frog Lake dam and some others along the upper section of Middle Ridge Trail.

Ground Iris

One of the most charming flowers in the park is also one of the smallest. The blossoms of purple mouse ears look like tiny, deep purple mouse faces with brilliant magenta ears. If you look inside the dark purple flower tube, you'll see bright golden stripes and striking yellow anthers. The plants grow only two or three inches tall, so it's easy to walk right past them without seeing them. Look for them in rocky areas with sparse vegetation along Corral Trail and Monument Trail. You might have to get down on your belly to really appreciate the beauty of the tiny flowers, but the rewards are well worth the effort. Some years, you won't find purple mouse ears anywhere,

Purple Mouse Ears

but during the El Nino spring of 1998, we found them growing by the hundreds, maybe even thousands, and in areas where we had never seen them before.

Bird's eye gilias often blanket large areas of hillsides with a pale blue glow. The petals are a whitewashed shade of blue, and the flower tube has alternating stripes of deep blue violet and bright yellow, which gives the flower its other common name, tricolor gilia. You can delight in the color the flowers give to the hillsides, but this is another one of those belly flowers; to really appreciate them, you need to get down to their level. When you do, you can see one of their most striking features, five fluffy azure blue anthers. The flowers have a strong fragrance that some people think is wonderful and other people find a little overwhelming. Look for bird's eye gilias along the road to the park growing in the hilly meadows a mile or two below the entrance. If you want to get up close to these wonderful little flowers, look for the small patch that grows on the east side of Hobbs Road just after it leaves Manzanita Point Road and starts up steeply towards the monument.

California Gilia

The California (or blue) gilia is a taller, forest dwelling relative of the bird's eye gilia. It's an easy plant to find. All you need to do is walk along the Corral Trail and look for fluorescent little blue globes straining to reach above the grass.

When you're hiking through some of the drier areas of the park, you might find Bitterroot, one of the rarest and loveliest flowers in the park. Bitterroot is a low-growing plant with a large, many-petaled flower in the middle of a ring of succulent, tube-shaped leaves. The petals of the flower vary in color from white to pink. A few small colonies that grow in the Miller Field and East Fork areas have beautiful translucent, iridescent pink petals. Because the plant was first described by Captain Lewis of the Lewis and Clark Expedition, botanists named it Lewisia.

I think my favorite spring wildflower is the white mariposa lily. Mariposa is the Spanish word for butterfly, and these showy tulip-like flowers do resemble butterflies. Although the petals are usually white with bright red markings on the inner surface, you'll sometimes find flowers with brighter colors, ranging from light red to brilliant crimson. A patch of red-flowered "white" mariposa lilies grows along the road to Poverty Flat, less than a mile from Coyote Creek. Each year, I look forward to seeing mariposa lilies, but they also make me a bit wistful since their presence is a sign that spring will soon be over.

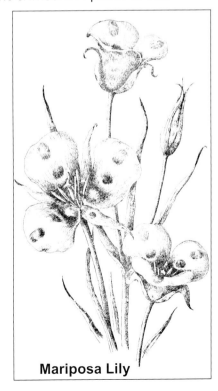

Mariposa Lily

There are two more common flowers that bloom for a long time and are well known by most Californians. One is our official state flower, the California poppy. Its peak blooming period is in middle to late spring, but you might find a poppy in bloom in July or February or almost any other month of the year.

Spring

The beauty of a poppy is in its simplicity. Its petals are not tri-colored, not bi-colored; they are simply the most beautiful shade of golden orange. A field of them can brighten your day, but to get the full effect, get down on your knees and peer into just one flower backlit by the sun. It can give you a new appreciation for all flowers.

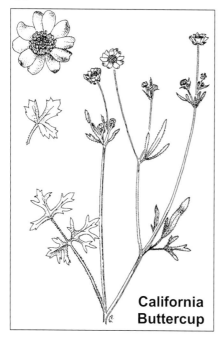

California Buttercup

The other long-lasting flower is the California buttercup. Buttercups are one of the earliest of the wildflowers, yet they can still have blossoms when the last of the spring flowers are beginning to fade.

Several days ago I sat down next to a buttercup and spent some time with it. As I looked into its bright shiny yellow face, I found intricate details that I'd never imagined such a "plain" little flower could have. It was no longer simply a buttercup; it was a living creature that had as much individuality as any person. As I spent more time with the buttercup, I realized that its existence was just as important as the existence of an ant, a sequoia, or any other living thing. I gained more respect for all life and more insight into my connection with the buttercup and all the other inhabitants of this earth.

The Emerald Chain

An old friend and I have had an ongoing difference of opinion. The poor guy's green with envy because I've seen so many beautifully colored rattlesnakes. The first piece below is from an article my deprived friend wrote for the July 1992 issue of The Ponderosa. *The second piece is a reply I wrote for* The Ponderosa *in the fall of that year. Here we are, many moons later, and The Great Green Rattlesnake Debate is still going strong.*

❖　❖　❖　❖　❖　❖　❖　❖　❖　❖

What Color are the Rattlesnakes in Coe Park—Really?

by Lee Dittmann

A usually reliable contributor to The Ponderosa has claimed on a number of occasions that the majority of rattlesnakes which inhabit Henry W. Coe State Park are green. As recently as the June 1989 issue, Ranger Breckling asserted, "...most of our rattlesnakes are a greenish color." This assertion has been assumed correct by many Park Volunteers and reported to the public as the true situation here. But is it?

Up until two years ago, yours truly had seen only three rattlers during his visits to Coe Park. All three were tan or otherwise light brown. Were these merely exceptions to the general rule of green rattlesnakes? This seemed possible—but since that time, I have had the good fortune of at least six additional sightings, including one dead snake on the Bell Station road. All of these were tan or brown, with one exception: one individual was banded tan and olive drab. That's olive drab, mind you, not olive green--the former color as much brownish as greenish. Casual inquiries of other Coe Park explorers revealed that they, too, had seen few, if any, green rattlesnakes. For example, at the Fall 1990 Volunteer Ride-along, Larry Haimowitz revealed that although he had always heard that most were green, he personally hadn't seen any.

What then, is Ranger Breckling's claim based upon? He tells me that in his fourteen years at Coe Park, he has seen an estimated 70 to 100 rattlers here and he remembers only two that weren't green. When pressed he states that, "Less than ten percent, anyway" were some color other than greenish. Does Barry Breckling see only green rattlers and ignore the rest? Have non-green rattlesnakes become more common in the last few years? Do I and a few others have some weird karmic mental block blinding us to that myriad of green vipers which are allegedly the predominant variation among poisonous slitherers at Coe? What's going on here?

❖ ❖ ❖ ❖ ❖ ❖ ❖ ❖ ❖ ❖

She was beautiful. Her skin was soft and smooth, her eyes catlike. Her slender body moved in slow, graceful undulations as the summer sun set, casting an orange tint on her moistureless yet shiny skin. In the light of day, her skin revealed beautiful patterns in hues of brown and tan, but the predominant color was a soft, earthy green, and today her colors were particularly lustrous because she had just shed.

Despite her beauty, many people were greatly repulsed by her kind. They failed to perceive her loveliness; they saw her only as an emissary of death, a poisonous viper hiding in the grass, waiting in ambush for human prey. If only they could know her thoughts. She felt no hatred, no anger. She simply felt a desire to survive and carry on her kind. Someday she would die, but her life would not have been in vain. She lived to a higher purpose. Her existence was as perennial as the grass. She formed a link in the emerald chain.

She'd spent the last winter by herself in a pile of rocks at the bottom of Kelly Cabin Canyon, unlike her relatives in the high mountains who denned in groups. One morning, after the April weather had warmed the canyon bottom and graced the verdant slopes with flowers, she left her den in search of food and a mate. She crawled up the hillside, away from the creek, and moved slowly through the low green grass. Before long, she came upon a male rattlesnake. They engaged in a quiet, graceful courtship, entwining their sleek bodies for a short time, and then departed on their separate ways. Fertilization of her eggs would take place later, and it would be many months before the young would be born.

She spent most of the spring looking for food in the warmth of the sun. In late May, on days when the ground warmed to over 80 degrees, she spent more time in the shade. If she were exposed to hot sunlight or sun-baked ground for even a few minutes, she could quickly overheat and die. On a hot June afternoon, a man and a woman sat down and began to eat their lunch less than two feet from a low shrub where she

The Emerald Chain

was hiding from the sun. She was only slightly concerned with their presence until the man saw her and reacted. He jumped up, knocking over a plastic bottle of lime drink and spilling a jar of olives. She quickly but quietly moved on.

Now, on a dark evening at the end of summer, she waited silently. Her only movement was an occasional flick of her tongue, which had told her much earlier that she was at the right place—the edge of a ground squirrel run. The pupils of her eyes, which were narrowed to slits during the day, were now wide open, and she could see the form of a young ground squirrel as it returned to its den. She had first detected the squirrel with her two heat-sensing pits, which were located slightly below and to the outside of her nostrils. As the squirrel approached, her heat sensors registered its distance and direction, and her brain translated the information into an infrared-like image of the animal.

At precisely the right time and with just the right amount of venom she struck. The terrified squirrel dashed off, which caused the venom to pump quickly through its body.
She slowly followed the scent of the squirrel, using her nose and tongue to track it as surely as a bloodhound. Her slender form allowed her to enter the narrow tunnel into which the squirrel had fled.

Even before the squirrel died, the venom had begun to digest its flesh. When she found its body, she moved the squirrel around until she got its head in her mouth. Unhooking her lower jaw, she began to swallow the animal, even though its body was larger than her mouth. Her backward-pointing teeth made the one-way trip possible, and rather than pulling the squirrel into her mouth, she inched forward and engulfed it with her own body.

Her belly would bulge for several days and she would move very little during that time. The meal would provide sufficient nourishment for more than a week. The young, inexperienced

squirrel had eaten the green spring grass and had in turn
been eaten by the graceful green snake. All three were links
in the emerald chain.

One fall afternoon, she was preparing to shed her skin for the
third time during the year and acquire her third new rattle of
the year. A small herd of elk moved toward the shade of the
large oak where she rested. She felt the ground vibrate as the
enormous animals approached. Under normal circumstances,
the situation would have been frightening enough, but her
fear was compounded by the fact that she was temporarily
blinded because she was about to shed. She vibrated her
rattles as hard as she could, and the resulting buzz—certainly
not a rattle—sent the elk galloping off.

She stayed close to the tree during the next few days.
The bulge she now had in her belly was not food; it was ten
embryonic snakes that were six to eleven inches long and still
encased in their eggs. Many species of snakes lay eggs, but
her eggs opened inside her and her young were born live.
They too were beautiful. Two were colored in pastel shades
of brown and tan, but the other eight looked more like their
mother, with soft green shades to their skin. The scientific
name that was chosen for her species, *Crotalus viridis*, reflects
her coloration; *viridis* is a Latin word for the color green.

The lives of her offspring would be hard, and just as their
mother had played her part in keeping the flow of nature
in balance, some of them would give up their lives to the
balance. A kingsnake would catch one. In self-defense, the
little rattlesnake would inject venom deep in the kingsnake's
body, but the effort would be in vain because kingsnakes are
immune to rattlesnake venom. Two of the young snakes would
become food for red-tailed hawks, and another would be eaten
by a scrub jay. Two of them would die during the winter
because they would be unable to find enough food to make
it through hibernation. One would be beaten with a stick and
crushed to death with a rock.

The Emerald Chain

Of her ten offspring, three would emerge from their dens in April, looking for food and mates. They too would play their parts in perpetuating the emerald chain.

Legend of the Oak

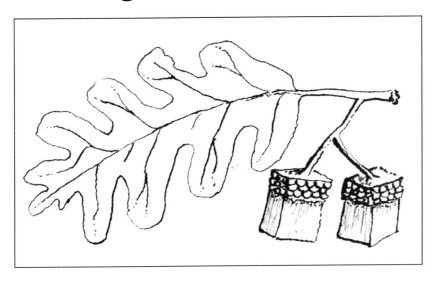

Once upon a time, a very long time ago, a grove of oak trees lived in a pretty little valley tucked deep in the mountains. A clear creek flowed down through the grove all year long, providing the trees with plenty of water. These trees were special, and they seemed to know it, for they were the only oak trees in the whole wide world. If you could have seen the grove in the winter or spring, you probably would have thought that the oaks were exactly like many of the oaks you see today, but if you'd seen them during the fall, you would have noticed something strange indeed. The acorns on the trees were big and square.

Very few of the acorns ever became trees. Occasionally one would land in a spot with just enough moisture and just enough light, and a new oak seedling would sprout. And every now and then a tired old oak would die and give a lucky little seedling the room it needed to grow up and become a respected member of the group. But, for the most part, the grove remained constant and contented, with few signs of change. The big square acorns never fell far from the trees and the little cluster of oaks never had more than about two dozen trees in their prime.

The Legend of the Oak

One year an acorn fell into just the right kind of spot, and a tiny new seedling popped out of the ground. Although the seedling looked and acted quite ordinary, deep down inside it held a secret. The little oak grew healthy and strong, and it kept its secret until the summer of its 16th year. That was the year when the tree made its first acorns, and its acorns were very strange indeed. These acorns were not your normal tough-skinned large acorns. No, these new acorns had thin skins and were small. But the most surprising thing of all was the shape of the acorns. They were round.

The other oaks were amazed by the acorns, and some of the younger trees laughed and made fun. The older trees were more polite, of course, but they were sure that such strange little acorns could never become trees.

One bright morning that fall, the oaks began to drop their acorns. Most of the acorns landed in spots that were less than ideal. They would lie still without sprouting and would slowly rot away. One of the acorns fell into a squirrel's hole, but the annoyed squirrel pushed it back out and kicked it away. A noisy jay swooped through the grove, but it barely even

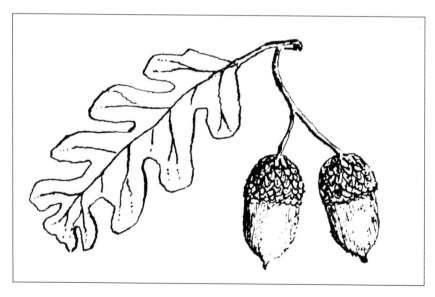

glanced at the acorns lying on the ground. The squirrels and the jays knew by their noses that the tasty meat inside the acorns would be yummy to eat, but they also knew that the acorns were too big and awkward to get a good grip on and that their tough shells were simply too hard to crack.

Later that morning, two young squirrels scampered around the grove playing hide and seek in the trees. One of them found a little round acorn, picked it up in its mouth, and carried it off to its favorite stump. It chipped away the thin shell and gobbled up the meat inside. Soon both squirrels were busy hunting for more of the tender acorns. A scrubby young jay happened along and noticed the commotion. He picked up one of the little acorns in his beak and flew up to the top of an old oak tree. Holding the round acorn steady with both feet, he chipped the outside shell away, ate the tasty meat inside, and gave out a loud boastful screech. News of the acorns spread quickly, and many more squirrels and jays soon joined in the feast. After a while, one by one, the animals began to get full. The squirrels tucked acorns into their cheeks and headed off in different directions to bury the acorns so that they could dig them up and eat them later. The jays flew off with acorns, stashed them in hastily dug holes here and there, and returned for more.

Before long, there were no more little round acorns lying on the ground, and some of the oak trees snickered a bit. But, unlike humans, squirrels and jays don't always remember where they put things, and the next spring several little oak seedlings popped out of the ground on the hillsides surrounding the valley. A few years passed, and each spring more oak trees graced the hillsides and spread into neighboring valleys. All the oaks outside the grove had little round acorns, and the oaks in the old grove no longer laughed at the strange oak tree in their midst.

❖ ❖ ❖ ❖ ❖ ❖ ❖ ❖ ❖ ❖ ❖

The Legend of the Oak

Some bright fall day, if you're exploring deep in the mountains, you may come across a hidden little valley with a clear stream flowing through it, and oaks all around. And if you look very carefully you might discover a few lonely old oaks trees with very strange acorns indeed.